Customer Service: How to Do It Right!

A Do-It-Yourself Strategy to Keep Your Customers Loyal, Attract New Ones and Increase Your Profits

by Peggy Morrow

A Southern Mountains Press Book

1

"As a leader, you have choices in taking your organization to a higher level of customer awareness in order to get and keep your customers. You can hire an expensive outside consultant or you can follow the guidelines of Peggy's book. It is all in these pages. Find a leader in your organization and go to it."

Irvin (Bubba) Levy, CEO, RSI.

"Excellent customer service is integral to success in any environment, particularly in an industry that is rapidly changing and facing competition. The way that people use libraries, perform research, and gather information has changed since the advent of the Internet, making customer service and added value from librarians even more important as people wade through a barrage of information.

Peggy Morrow's deep knowledge of customer service has helped raise standards of service at the Fondren Library. Her new book outlines a very practical approach to implementing improved customer service strategies in an organization. From experience in working with Peggy, and using the ideas outlined in her book "Customer Service: How to Do It Right!," our library has developed a multi-pronged approach, including obtaining customer feedback, training in how to deal with angry customers, hiring tips, and motivational techniques. This book will serve as a future benchmark in keeping us on track as we continue to work on improving our customer service."

Sara Lowman
Director of Fondren Library
Rice University

"Peggy Morrow most effectively covers the dynamics of customer service and offers insights, practical suggestions and work tools so needed for patient retention in today's ever changing world of healthcare delivery. Comprehensive, thorough and effective, this book is the perfect resource for anyone who wants to fine tune their service procedures. Thank you for empowering us to be our own consultants."

Arlene Weinberg M.H.A, C.M.P.E.
Practice Administrator
Katy-West Houston OB/GYN Associates

"Peggy's knowledge and training has assisted our managers and staff with maintaining our high service standards as well as continuing to develop our culture of service. This book gives everyone the opportunity to learn from her philosophy on training."

Paul Schultz
Managing Director
The San Luis Resort, Spa & Conference Center

Customer Service: How to Do It Right!

A Do-It-Yourself Strategy to Keep Your Loyal Customers, Attract New Ones and Increase Your Profits

A Southern Mountains Press Book 2005

ISBN: 0-9723963-3-0
Library of Congress: 2004117499
Cover Design: Whitney Campbell & Co., Advertising & Design, wcdesign@maine.rr.com

The author, Peggy Morrow, is available for consultations, seminars and speaking engagements. Contact Peggy Morrow at: 800-375-1982, peggy@peggymorrow.com or via her Web page, www.peggymorrow.com.

Southern Mountains Press
4608 Compass Rose
Suite #24

Vermilion, OH 44089
440-963-0099
www.southernmountainspress.com

Introduction

Customer Service is always an important subject for most small and medium size businesses, knowing that it can give them a competitive edge over large corporate chains. In fact, one would guess that it is so important that virtually all businesses from mom and pop shops to local franchise owners would have specific plans in place to make superior customer service happen in their organizations.

Unfortunately, that is not true. In fact, the lack of attention to this one simple and critical aspect of business has kept me very busy as a consultant, speaker and newspaper columnist for over 22 years, creating programs for companies as diverse as National Football League Houston Texans, Baseball's Houston Astros, Rice University, Texas Medical Center, Shell Products, Toyota and many small businesses.

Along the way, I've discovered that all businesses, no matter what their size, have similar problems implementing effective customer service. Given how vital every dollar is in the competitive marketplace, it is crucial that these problems be solved or reversed. Despite high employee turnover, limited training budgets and far too few hours in the day, solutions do exist.

My message is simple—you don't have to hire an expensive consultant to develop a program in your business that will make customer service your competitive edge. You can "do it yourself" with the help of the step-by-step process detailed in this book. It's easy to talk about customer service in an abstract way; however, this book divides the process into doable steps that will help you retain your customers, attract new ones and be more profitable.

Competitive-edge customer service—shaped to your business's needs—will help you earn more money and increase growth and market share. Even better news—the methods you will learn in this book require little or no capital investment, apply to virtually every business and can immediately make a healthier bottom line.

This book offers these very specific benefits for every business owner:

1. A step-by-step plan to make implementing effective customer service in your company easy. It goes far beyond simply putting your employees through a "smile and be nice course." Easy-to-understand directions, how-to lists and

guides and extensive checklists give you the tools you will need to establish and maintain a profitable customer service strategy.

2. A plan to seek better hires, orient and train your employees so you will have less turnover and, thus, be able to offer consistently excellent customer service.

3. Improved profitability. A Bain & Company study found that a business with a real annual growth of 2.5 percent can triple growth and increase profits 25 percent by retaining an additional 5 percent of its customer base per year.

4. Increased loyalty of your customers, especially the high value ones. Research by David M. Szymanski, JC Penney Chair of Retailing Studies and Director of the Center for Retailing Studies in the Mays Business School at Texas A&M University, shows that highly committed customers are more loyal customers, more likely to spread the word about their positive experiences and more forgiving of the company when mistakes occur. A loyal customer can be worth thousands of dollars over the course of their transactions with you, since it takes five to six times as much effort to attract a new customer as it does to keep an old one.

5. Building of a strong brand, established in part by the experience your customer has with your business.

6. Customers often base their first buying decision on price, but buy the second time based on service, so you can usually charge higher prices.

7. Less stress in your job because, when your employees can handle customers well, it results in a more cooperative work environment and fewer angry customers.

8. The ability to establish methods of listening to your customers. You can monitor continuous customer feedback to use in delivering the level of service that turns your current customers into cheerleaders and attracts new customers.

Practical in nature and implementation, this book will lead you through the process of establishing a successful customer service program for your business. It will be an invaluable aid to help you make sure that you are delivering superior service to every customer, every time. Each chapter ends with a checklist or evaluation, so you can test your company's mastery of the information in that chapter.

In **Chapter One** you will learn how other companies are differentiating themselves through exceptional service, why service guarantees can help you stand out from the competition and ways you can add value to the customer's experience in order to increase loyalty. It concludes with a checklist to help you determine what elements you may be missing in your quest for achieving superior customer service.

Chapter Two discusses ideas for planting a culture of service—a most important step in creating competitive-edge service. It will also help you develop a service vision that you can use to focus everyone in your company on the customer, learn the importance of creating a climate of celebration and develop a program customized for your business.

Chapter Three emphasizes the importance of obtaining customer feedback on a regular basis and gives you ideas on initiatives to gather that feedback. It lists three basic elements you must learn about your service from your customers and offers sample questionnaires and a concluding checklist to help you with this most important step in achieving a service edge.

Communicating your expectations through service targets and stressing employee responsibility and accountability is the subject of **Chapter Four.** It will help you define in specific terms what "excellent service" looks like in your business and work you through the simple steps in the process.

Chapter Five discusses the importance of complaining customers and why and how complaints give you valuable feedback you can use to increase customer loyalty. You will learn the primary reasons customers get upset, so you can avoid them in your organization.

How to handle those complaining customers skillfully is the subject of **Chapter Six.** Through a step-by-step process, you will learn how to turn that angry customer into a loyal one and receive tips on how to control your own anger when dealing with these terrorist customers.

Chapter Seven discusses the importance of the hiring process in selecting employees who have a natural affinity for good customer service behaviors. It explains why you need to take as much care in hiring customer service employees as you would in selecting a high-level manager. It will help you develop questions and job specifications and guide you through the interview process. A quiz at the end will help you rate yourself on your hiring techniques.

Developing and delivering a powerful orientation program is the subject of **Chapter Eight.** It will show you how to develop an effective program that will get your employees pointed in the right direction and comfortable with their new job. You will learn whether or not your program contains all the common elements that make up a successful orientation process.

Chapter Nine shows you how spending the time to thoroughly train your employees can help you deliver the kind of service that will keep your customers loyal. It discusses the two general areas in which to provide training and how to develop the content for each.

Techniques for motivating your employees to consistently deliver excellent service and developing the "want to" factor are discussed in **Chapter Ten.** Ways to create a climate of motivation and examples of both internal and external motivators are discussed. Over fifty different ideas for motivation are provided. Rate yourself with the "How Good Are You at Motivation?" quiz.

Chapter Eleven shares tips on coaching employees to improved performance. It helps you decide whether it is a knowledge, skill or attitude problem and provides techniques you can use in each circumstance. It also gives you a step-by-step process you can use when employees don't do what they have been taught to do and the four possibilities for performance improvement.

Retention of your employees is another key to achieving a consistent level of exceptional service, and **Chapter Twelve** discusses the Five Rs that will plant a culture of retention in your business to keep your employees working for you longer. It helps you create a "total employment experience" that goes way beyond a paycheck.

Chapter Thirteen helps you see that the process discussed in the book doesn't have to take a lot of time. It will make you aware of some of the forces that will affect customer service in the future, so you can plan your next steps in developing a customer service initiative that will help you grow your profits.

The **Appendixes** give you some specific tools to use while developing your own approach to doing customer service right!

This book is filled with stories from the trenches. They are included to show the positive methods that will help the reader discover what can be done, despite obstacles that you think cannot be overcome. The promise of this book is, by following this step-by-step approach, your business can use customer service to keep your loyal customers, attract new ones and increase your profits.

Peggy Morrow

Foreword

Much has been written about the inevitable commoditization of products. Actually, it is quite clear that without some form of differentiation, most products will eventually be evaluated and selected by consumers using price as the key discriminating factor. However, creating a unique overall customer experience through outstanding service is one of the most important ways to protect your product from becoming a commodity in our fast-paced, 24/7 society.

In this book, Peggy Morrow lays out a simple, straightforward and action-oriented approach to developing a customer service strategy that can be immediately applied to your organization. Peggy has taken her experience with hundreds of businesses (like the Houston Texans) across many industries and extracted a set of principles that can be universally applied. Just like most things in customer service, the principles and applications contained in this book are not difficult to understand, but they are very difficult to master.

It is important to note that Customer Service is not a program, a department or an approach to overcome a poor quality product. Rather, to succeed, customer service must become a value system embraced and espoused by the highest levels of a company and practiced relentlessly throughout the organization. In this book, Peggy takes us through the various components of a world class customer service program:

- Creating the Culture

- Attracting the Right People

- Training for Excellence

- Measuring Performance

- Motivation & Retention

Successful implementation of these principles will take a total, organization-wide commitment to outstanding service, but I can tell you from experience the results are well worth the effort. Mastering customer service within any company can deliver many tangible and strategic benefits. Great customer service can:

- Enhance your profit margins because consumers are willing to pay more for products with a great service and experiential component

- Protect your customer base through increased retention

- Increase your revenue potential through related sales to existing customers

- Build your brand through positive word of mouth, which is usually more credible and persuasive than paid advertising

- Increase your sales through direct referrals

Most importantly, your employees will take greater pride in your company and their work because they know the organization is a trusted and respected friend to their customers. They will feel that their mission is not simply to generate a profit, but rather to serve and fulfill the needs of another human being. This sense of purpose is great inspiration for most employees.

You should also know that the impacts of outstanding customer service are most readily achievable for small businesses. Small companies do not have to be all things to all people. They can usually customize their product and service offering so that it appears to be perfectly designed for the target audience. This customization of offering is a key competitive weapon against larger rivals who usually come armed with a healthy cost advantage. And when things do not go right, a small business knows pretty quickly and they can respond to meet the needs of their customers. However, great customer service on any level starts with a commitment from the company and its leadership. So, are you up to the challenge?

I hope you enjoy this book as much as we have enjoyed delighting the fans of the Houston Texans through the application of the principles contained within it.

Jamey Rootes
Senior Vice President,
NFL Houston Texans

Acknowledgments

Writing a book is never easy. But with the help of many people, it has become a reality. Thank you to Larry Chilnik at Southern Mountains Press who shepherded me through the process and to my editors Lauri Stash and Norma Collins for their careful editing of the manuscript.

To all my clients and colleagues who supported and assisted, thank you. Without you, I wouldn't have the experience and knowledge necessary to write this book. Thank you, too, to Debra Bailey for her invaluable research assistance, Mel Kleiman for his time and ideas he shared with me, and John Goodman of Technical Assistance Research Programs (TARP) for his review of data.

And most of all, to my wonderful husband, Tommy, who encouraged me throughout the whole process.

Customer Service: How to Do It Right!

A Do-It-Yourself Strategy to Keep Your Customers Loyal, Attract New Ones and Increase Your Profits

by Peggy Morrow

CONTENTS

CHAPTER ONE

Customer Service—The Key to Your Competitive Edge

Few small or medium size business owners today are unaware of the importance of good customer service. Given the financial leverage of the larger businesses, will customer service be enough to keep your business flourishing, or even growing, in these exceptionally competitive times?

This book asserts that it can be. *Customer Service: How to Do It Right!* shows you exactly how to integrate the right customer service program into your business with an easy step-by-step approach. When your company makes exceptional service happen for every customer, every time, you will become the company of choice for both your employees and your customers.

Here's an example:

Shortly after Bob and Glenda Johnson celebrated their 30th wedding anniversary, they took stock of their lives. Their house would be paid off in one year, their kids were long gone and had their own lives. Plus, they could actually see a time, not too far in the future, when they could take time for themselves. Glenda, having taught for 27 years could retire anytime, and since Bob was a consultant he made his own schedule.

As they reviewed their finances, they realized that all their insurance (homeowners, car and life) was all with one company. Each night Bob watched the financial news become more complicated—actually downright depressing—and he wondered if it was time to get a financial planner so that their security would not be compromised.

Bob called his insurance broker plus several others. Bob and Glenda met with different people and were offered different plans that everyone said would make money. Their own agent also had a plan—but it wasn't significantly different from other firms' offerings.

The truth was that Bob and Glenda weren't sure what to do. So they made the decision based on one factor. Their agent had served them well for 30 years. He had always returned their phone calls promptly and any claims they submitted were paid promptly. He now had a financial planner in his office, so they decided to use those services and stay with the agent's firm because he could guarantee one thing: value through good service.

I hear this story far more today than "I'm just looking for the best price" when I interview customers about their experiences. In this case, service was the differentiating factor. Not that price is not still an issue; but more and more customers are looking for low prices **plus** the value that service brings to the transaction. You must have both today if you want to succeed.

But delivering outstanding customer service doesn't have to be expensive. Most changes you will make to improve service require little or no cost.

As you will learn from this book, if you are going to succeed as a small or medium size business today, and possibly expand, you must make the delivery of exceptional customer service a very large part of the equation. It must become part of the way you do things. Delivering outstanding customer service is essential when competing with the "big boys." Gone are the days when you could compete on price or unique product alone. Even if you have a unique product or idea, other businesses—especially the superstores—quickly follow your lead on price and will rapidly copy your innovations.

Just look at some of these findings across numerous industries from various sources, including the Canadian Marketing Association and the National Federation of Independent Business:

- Twelve good service experiences are required to overcome a single bad one.

- One dollar spent on advertising yields less than $5 in incremental revenue, but that same dollar spent on improving customer service can yield more than $60 in incremental revenue.

- Seventy-five percent of all e-shopping carts are abandoned before the purchase is actually completed. Nine out of ten shoppers who abandoned their carts did so because of a lack of customer service.

In addition, research from TARP (Technical Assistance Research Programs) found that:

- Ninety-one percent of unhappy customers will never buy again from a company that displeased them.

- Ninety-five percent of your customers will stay if their problems are fixed correctly.

- Excellent service leads to increased margins. TARP has found that people are willing to spend up to 15% more for excellent service for the same product.

- Customer loyalty will drop by about 20% if the customer has encountered a problem.

Other studies report that good service contributes to a company being chosen as a preferred vendor, and as companies get to know their customers better, cross sales of new products also increase.

One vital result of a customer service focus is that referral customers, who cost nothing to acquire and usually arrive already decided to buy, often come as the result of good service.

- One hardware store estimated as much as 50% of its sales are from referrals, and this enables them to generate enough business to go up against the "big box" hardware stores. They stock hard-to-find items and are known for their friendly, knowledgeable sales staff.

Differentiation through Service

The quality of service you offer is one of the few ways you can market your product or service as being significantly different from the competition. Few companies can offer something truly unique. Face it, most competitors are selling the same things with very little to tell their products or services apart. If price and product quality are about equal, the only real difference is how customers' needs are met through the quality of service you offer.

Sam Greengard, writing in *Chief Executive Magazine*, tells how Christopher Milliken, CEO of OfficeMax, a Boise Company, recognized the only way to escape the bruising price competition and razor-thin margins of office supply superstores was to provide greater value and superior customer service. Milliken invested a serious amount of money into a revolutionary customer relationship management program that enables his business to stand out from the others in the area of customer service. This helps Boise/OfficeMax cross-market, cross-sell and service accounts more effectively.

Here are ways that small and medium size businesses are differentiating their organizations through exceptional service.

- An office supply company visits their customers monthly and checks on levels of service satisfaction. They also inform the customers of new products and services as well as changes to the company Web site. One customer relates, "This has probably been the biggest factor in my choosing them as our primary source. I feel they care about our business."

- A small grocery store caters to its elderly customers by boxing purchases and loading them in their cars and by carrying personal charge accounts for their customers. They also send their customers holiday greeting cards.

- A party rental store allows the customers to move around the decorative items they are considering renting until they get a good feel for the final look of the rented items.

- A safety alarm company answers its phone the old fashioned way—with a real person. They don't force their customers to use an automated system and they always return calls within 24 hours.

- A successful nail salon that recently expanded to two locations is open seven days a week so they can be easily accessible to their customers. They also deliver something extra—an exceptionally long massage when doing a customer's nails.

Here's another success story of a company that has built a successful business based on excellence in customer service.

Space Center Tire and Auto, a full-service auto repair and tire facility, put the focus on its customer and has built its business from zero to $3.5 million in three years. The count of cars serviced has increased 20 percent a year, now averaging 60-80 cars per day.

After starting and managing several similar businesses for others, owner Todd McIntosh felt that everyone should be able to get good service for their vehicle. "Not everyone can afford a Cadillac, Lexus or BMW and the exceptional service that it brings," he emphasizes. "I wanted to make affordable service available to everyone."

And he has done just that. His customer service rating, as tracked on a weekly basis, is consistently 97 percent and higher. He believes this measurement is one of the keys to his exceptional success in a business with a traditionally poor reputation for service.

He measures the level of his service in many ways.

When customers' cars are delivered after the service is performed, they will find an evaluation hangtag asking, "Tell us how we are doing so we can serve you better." It consists of five items for the customer to rate from poor to excellent. He then rewards his employees based on that rating. He posts the results and distributes rewards weekly, because he believes that rewards spaced too far apart are not motivating enough.

His goals are challenging, yet realistic. Employees must get a rating of 98 percent in order to receive the largest incentive. McIntosh feels that 100 percent is almost impossible because, "There are some people you just can't please."

He also measures his service through yearly focus groups comprised of women, because 70 percent of car repair work is done for women. He has learned ways to make sure his female customers don't feel "talked down to" by carefully explaining each procedure and avoiding jargon.

Still another way he tracks service to ensure that his customers return is to call them 24–48 hours after the service so they can rate the experience. This is also filtered into the incentive system.

Individual acts of exceptional service are also rewarded. Recently one employee went out of his way and picked up a sick customer's car, had the service performed, and then returned the car to the customer. He was praised and rewarded with a dinner for him and his spouse.

"Our success is not based on sales but on service, and we are always trying to do it better," he emphasizes. McIntosh truly believes that if you take care of the customers and give them exceptional service, the money will follow. And it certainly has. His vision of everything flowing from the customer and "Giving Auto Service a Good Name" is the principle with which he guides his extremely successful efforts.

Service Guarantees

Another way you can use customer service as your differentiator and competitive edge is to offer a service guarantee. Customers are loyal to companies they trust, so build trust by ensuring that customers know the business will stand behind its service and honor its commitments.

Guarantees can put teeth into, and make customers believe, that the advertisements about your exceptional service are true. A promise of payment or solution when failures occur can impact your bottom line in a positive way.

Many companies are afraid to offer a free service guarantee for fear they can't deliver on it and it will cost them too much. But promising perfect service forces a company to actually deliver it or else come as close as they can. It serves as a good tool and goal to help employees meet your customers' expectations. It sets service targets or standards for your employees and yourself to live up to. Guarantees also encourage employees to do the job right the first time.

Darla Haygood, Vice President of Marketing and Business Development at Meador Staffing Services Inc., says they promise clients they don't have to pay if they are disappointed with the performance of its employees, even if their reason for the dissatisfaction does not surface for several weeks. The company says this promise of satisfaction is one of the reasons their rate of sales growth has outstripped the average growth rate for similar businesses.

Debra Schindler, President of Genesis Telecom, designs, installs, services and maintains communication systems. She tells the story of starting her business in 1983 during a very challenging business environment. "I knew I had to do something different," she says. So she decided to guarantee a one-hour emergency response time. If her company didn't follow through, she made the customer's next monthly payment if they were on a contract or gave them credit to be used for other services or hardware.

In order to make the guarantee happen, they implemented a system to track their trucks so they know where everyone is at all times. "When we get an emergency call, we check for traffic jams, route the closest truck around the problem and get help to the client within the guaranteed hour," says Schindler.

While a failure of your service guarantee can be expensive, it raises awareness and creates urgency for service improvement in order to prevent future failures. Service guarantees increase customer satisfaction and reduce complaints, which in turn will improve your bottom line. Creating service guarantees also drives a company to identify and solve the root causes of service-delivery problems like slow response or complaint resolution time.

A well-known example of a service guarantee driving service behaviors is FedEx, with its customer-driven standard of "absolutely, positively overnight." This tells their customers what to expect and employees what they must deliver in order to create customer trust and loyalty.

Loyalty

Keeping the customers you have is another key to using service as your competitive edge. If you are appealing to your customers solely on the basis of price, they will quickly go down the street when they find a lower price. Developing loyalty through exceptional service is critical to your organization's success.

A multi-industry study by the University of Pennsylvania's Wharton School of Business found that companies who managed to reduce their customer attrition by only 5 to 10 percentage points actually increased their profits by an astounding 25 to 75 percent, depending on the business.

The National Federation of Independent Business finds that 65 percent of a company's present business comes from existing customers and that it costs five times as much to attract a new customer as it does to keep an existing one. If you aren't actively pursuing a customer loyalty program, you will soon be out of business.

Obviously, highly satisfied customers are more likely to be loyal. But they must be *highly* satisfied, not just satisfied. Thomas O. Jones and W. Earl Sasser Jr., in a *Harvard Business Review* article, related how researchers found Xerox

Corporation's "totally satisfied" customers were six times more likely to repurchase the company's products over the following eighteen months than customers who rated themselves as merely "satisfied."

In other words, you must develop "delighted" and "enthusiastic" customers to keep them loyal to your product or service. They must be so impressed with the level of service they are receiving that they will turn into "cheerleaders" for you.

Knowing the value of your current customers is very important too. This helps you to see how critical their continued loyalty is to the success of your business.

Do you know the value of your current customers?

Use the following formula to calculate it:

A. $_____ How much does your average customer spend per transaction?

B. _____Multiply 'A' by the number of times that customer visits or patronizes your business each year.

C. _____Multiply 'B' times ten (this is the number of years a lifetime customer will stay with you. (C = B x 10)

D. _____A lifetime customer will bring you at least one additional customer through referral. (D = C x 2)

Now deduct the cost of getting and keeping that customer to determine the value of your average customer.

An example from a retail store:

A. Average customer transaction: $100

B. Number of time customer buys per year = 6
A x B = Average customer expenditure per year $600

C. $600 x 10 (B x 10) = average years a customer will
stay with you and their expenditures $6,000

D. One additional customer brought by your original
customer (lifetime value) $6,000

Cost of getting and keeping your original customer =   -$500
                                                                    _____

Total value of a current customer = $11,500

How did you do? Are your current customers worth more than you thought? Retaining your customers through delivery of excellent service is just as important as attracting new ones. Yet many businesses put all their efforts and most of their budget into getting new customers.

Kindercare Learning Centers estimate that each new customer they attract is worth $5000 over the life of that customer. If that customer leaves to go somewhere else because of poor service, it affects their profitability.

Remember: loyal, long-established customers are the most profitable because they buy more, refer new business and are often willing to pay slightly higher prices.

Ways to Inspire Customer Loyalty

- Develop programs to cultivate relationships and loyalty with prospective customers as early as possible. A strong competitive edge is gained if a relationship can be established before customers are even aware of the competition.

- Look for customers with new needs. For example, seek out residents who are new to the community or first-time homeowners. Look for families with new babies or new pets.

- Develop loyalty in children and teens. Start a teen advisory board if that is applicable to your business, or offer special amenities for children.

- A Mexican restaurant has cemented many of their customers' loyalty by offering a giant play area complete with sand box and lots of toys. Parents can easily watch over their children from the bar area. Soon their children are pleading to go back to this restaurant because it is such fun.

- Another restaurant provides chalk and allows children to write on the floor while they wait for dinner.

- Relationship-building programs like child sizes, toys with the company logo on them, sponsorship of children's events and anything that exposes children to your business will build long-term loyalty in both parents and children.

- Offering your customers a large range of products and services will also contribute to loyalty. A credit union pitches a whole package of financial products including savings accounts, credit cards, mortgage and car loans and IRAs. The larger the mix of the company's products and services a customer uses, the less likely that he will sever the relationship.

- Linda Truman, a successful Virtuoso specialist in the art of travel, is always helpful with all aspects of a trip, even if she gets no commission on parts of the arrangement. She will provide information about good taxi services or restaurants at the traveler's destination, even if there is nothing in it for her. Consequently, she has a long list of loyal customers.

Developing a customer loyalty program is an essential part of using customer service as your competitive edge. This book will help you assemble all the service elements you need to keep your customers coming back and even turn them into promoters for your company.

Deliver Customer Value

Another element that must be in place for service to be your competitive edge is the delivery of exceptional customer value. You must understand what your customers value most about your company or product and consistently deliver it so they remain loyal and turn into those cheerleaders I mentioned earlier. An often-used definition of value is "what you get for what you give, both monetary and nonmonetary." Another is "a thing is worth what it can do for you, not what you choose to pay for it."

Value has five elements:

- Quality
- Price
- Service
- Timeliness
- Innovation

Customers are becoming increasingly value-conscious. They automatically shop for value. They think about what they wanted, what they received, what its cost and whether they got their "money's worth." This behavior is rooted in the belief that price is not the only thing that matters. In order to use the delivery of excellent customer service to improve profitability, you must create customer value. You must discover what your customers want and will pay money for, and then align all your systems and procedures to deliver that.

When you don't discover what your customers value, you waste money delivering the wrong things—things that don't really add value to the customers' experiences in their eyes. Or the opposite. You don't provide customers with what they think is most valuable.

For example, a healthcare clinic specializing in diagnostic imaging processes thought that patients most valued a warm and friendly staff. But, when they looked at their customer feedback, they found that the ease of getting a fast and convenient appointment was more important to them, and the warm and friendly factor was 5th on the list.

A major grocery chain store manager told a customer that he had recently visited a rival grocery store and found the store less clean than his own and with fruit flies in the produce area. "So why do they have more business than us?" queried the manager. "Our store is cleaner, and we don't have fruit flies." "Because the staff is friendlier, and their produce is better, even with fruit flies," replied the customer. "I will put up with fruit flies to get better produce and friendlier people." The store manager was delivering the wrong values. He thought a clean store was what his customers wanted, while in reality they wanted friendly service and better produce, more than a clean store.

Milton W. Ellisor, President of Polyspec LLC, founded his business on the premise that they would deliver superior service **as defined by the customer.** He felt his competitors were not delivering the service customers really wanted, so he started his own company dedicated to discovering and then delivering the right level of service. He differentiated his business and became very successful based in part on that one element.

In his book, *Competitive Advantage: Creating and Sustaining Superior Performance,* Michael Porter writes, "Competitive advantage grows fundamentally out of the value a firm is able to create for its buyers." So spend some time discovering what matters to your customers. What do they value enough to make them want to do business with you and not your competitors?

One way to do this is to listen for "I wish" statements by your customers. "I wish you were open on Sundays." "I wish you would combine these two forms to make it faster to complete." "I wish this didn't have to take so long." These types of statements will give you good ideas of ways that you can add extra value to your customers' experiences.

Southwest Airlines is great at this. They carefully listen to customer complaints and wishes and then change their systems and procedures to make it happen. The check- in procedure, for instance, has been tweaked many times to make it easier and faster for their customers.

Which elements do your customers value enough to keep coming back and even pay more money for? If it is service or a combination of service and the other attributes, you must constantly be improving in that area. Why? Because your competitors are! How does your company measure up?

How Can Your Company Add Value to Your Customer's Experience?

- A tire and automobile repair shop washes each customer's car before it is returned. They also have a free van service that will take the customer to work or home after dropping off the car. Then it picks them up when the work is finished.

- A dry cleaner makes it a point to remember their regular customers' names and retrieves their cleaning as they walk in the door. This saves the customer time and makes them feel valued and important.

- A restaurant gives a small toy to each child regardless of what they order.

- A bank found their customers want to wait no longer than four minutes in line to reach a teller. So they staffed their windows and drive-thrus so that customers wait no longer than three minutes on the average.

- After a customer purchases flowers or an arrangement, a florist surprises the customer with a single flower from her stock. It costs very little but makes a positive, lasting impression.

- A family-owned furniture store located in New Orleans, Louisiana, came up with a unique idea to enhance customer service and add a little value to each sale. First, emphasis is placed on making the sale a very positive experience and ensuring that completion of the sale is done in a manner that doesn't leave the customer with unanswered questions.

Since furniture is a major investment for many people, the sales staff assure the customer that if it "doesn't work" in their house or there is something wrong, the purchase is guaranteed. The store has also created a wall with a variety of art prints, framed posters and other decorative items. At the end of the transaction, customers are surprised and given a choice of a picture from the selection on the wall. The customer service message is clear. It's the store's way of giving their customer just a little something extra and adding a little value to the transaction. What customer wouldn't think warmly of that sale every time they see the picture?

- A dry cleaner guarantees their work and has a large, framed sign over its counter that reads: "We have such intense pride in our skills, workmanship and equipment that we guarantee everything. You must be completely satisfied, or we will do whatever is necessary to meet your expectations." A feeling of security about the service adds value in many customers' minds.

In each case above, the owners have **exceeded their customers' expectations in a small way and thus added value.** Surprising and delighting your customers with a little bit more than they expect is a key part of establishing loyalty and making them believe they are receiving exceptional value.

If that value-added extra is something that your competitors cannot duplicate easily, like immediate service response, unconditional guarantees, hassle-free financing or free parking, it will help cement your customer's loyalty and thus help your bottom line.

A plumbing company pledges to be there within 12 hours and also offers 24/7 service. When you have water all over your kitchen floor from the dishwasher, this is a significant service point.

In order for your efforts to pay off, you must let your customers know about your special service. Post signs, include notes with their bills, and tell them about it. A small, independent grocery store has a little notice in each grocery bag touting the special handling of your groceries. It explains how they keep all the frozen food together, handle produce gently, and don't make the bags too heavy to carry.

Too many companies are concentrating on low prices and not considering that customers want more than just low prices. In fact, today's customers expect low prices **and** extra value. So in order to stay competitive, you must understand how the service part of the value equation fits into how you offer value to your customer.

How Are You Currently Doing?

Do you have all the elements in place to make superior customer service happen? Use this checklist to rate your company.

1.	Do you measure your customer service on a regular basis?	Yes	No
2.	Is everyone's compensation, from the top down, tied to customer satisfaction?	Yes	No
3.	Do you know your customers' lifetime value?	Yes	No
4.	Is your customer service message featured prominently in all customer communications, both internal and external?	Yes	No
5.	Is your budget for customer service-related activities a major part of your sales and marketing budget?	Yes	No
6.	Are <u>all</u> employees trained in the appropriate customer service skills for their position?	Yes	No
7.	Do you have written procedures for people to follow in the most common customer service situations?	Yes	No
8.	Do managers regularly visit and communicate with the employees who interface with your customers?	Yes	No
9.	Have your customers stopped shopping around or going to bid because they know you will take care of them?	Yes	No
10.	Have you recently won a job where your service reputation was a deciding factor?	Yes	No

11. Do you or someone else regularly call or shop your company to see how you are doing?　　　　Yes　　　No

12. Do you have a system to gather suggestions from those employees who have direct contact with your customers?　　　　Yes　　　No

Scoring

10-12 yeses: Your business is already doing a great job on making customer service your competitive-edge. Keep it up!

7-9 yeses: You are on the right track, but need some work on creating customer value, loyalty and differentiation through service.

Less than 7: You need to get serious about making outstanding customer service happen in your organization or you will soon be out of business. This book will cover all of the above concerns and even more.

Your entire operation must be aligned to meet and exceed customers' expectations in order to increase profitability. There is no magic bullet, no one thing that will improve your service enough for it to be your competitive-edge. You must create an entire "culture" of service that goes deeply into an organization and results in excellent service.

Growing a beautiful garden means planting the right seeds. Growing a successful business means planting the right seeds of service. In the next chapter, you will discover how this process works and how you can do it yourself.

CHAPTER TWO

Growing a Culture of Service—Five Steps

This may be very familiar:

"Get everyone customer service training now," bellows the frustrated manager. *"Our customer satisfaction ratings are WAY down."* Will this quick fix help improve customer service? Maybe. But that's not all that needs to happen.

Training your employees in the skills of how to treat customers is certainly an important part of being able to deliver consistently outstanding customer service. But training is only part of the equation. Your organization will not reach the next level until you consider how you can do something even more important. In order for service to be your competitive edge, **you must plant a culture of service in your organization**. It must be ingrained so deeply that everything about your processes, systems and people are focused on serving the customer.

Diane Ozzolek, Director of Customer Service for the NFL Houston Texans, says, "You must start at the top. Service must be a core principle of the organization with everyone on the same page." Texans owner, Bob McNair, is the first to step up. He passes on any positive letters he receives with a personal note of congratulations. He "walks the talk." Jamey Rootes, Senior Vice President of the NFL Houston Texans, says, "I want to change the way this industry provides service," and he is looking at all aspects of the experience and culture he controls in order to do that.

Ozzolek recommends constantly keeping the idea of customer service in front of everyone. "Anytime you discuss an aspect of the business like budgets, for instance, the service component must be considered and reinforced. Award service risk-takers, really applaud them and publicly recognize people." She emphasizes it is usually the things that don't cost a lot of money that make the difference in your culture.

Simply sending people to "training" or conducting seminars and retreats is putting the cart miles ahead of the horse. Here are five steps that will help you plant your own culture of service.

Step Number One: Management Must Lead the Way.

To plant a culture of service that will become your company's competitive edge, you must start at the top. This is where your own leadership comes into play. Management must lead the way and model the vision of superior service. If you say one thing but do another, no one will listen to you. It's like signaling right and turning left. Employees will always take their cue on how to treat the customer from their managers.

When a manager treats customers rudely or complains about them behind their backs, employees take note of this and soon exhibit the same behaviors. You must model a behavior towards customers that says: "The customer comes first, and they are the whole reason for the existence of the business."

How do you use your time?

- Do you spend most of your day locked up in your office wrestling with numbers?

- Or do you spend at least part of your time visiting the front line to ask their advice about how to better serve the customer?

- Do you occasionally serve the customer yourself?

When your employees see you talking to and otherwise caring for customers, they will imitate your behavior.

For some small company proprietors, this is a no-brainer. For example, Todd McIntosh, the owner of Space Center Tire and Auto mentioned earlier, knows that the early mornings and late afternoons are the busiest times in the shop. So during these times he works right alongside of his employees. This contact with employees not only gives him greater insight into his customers' needs, but also sends a strong message that customers are his most important priority.

Contrast that with the manager who solicits ideas from her employees on ways to improve customer service but then minimizes or ignores their contribution.

Have you ever observed a manager being nasty to a customer with a complaint and then making disparaging remarks about the customer when he leaves? Yet all around the customer areas are signs stating, "The customer comes first." What's an *employee* to believe? What they read or what they see? What do you think will happen the next time that employee has to deal with a complaint? A deeply embedded culture comes more from what you do than what you say. Will Rogers said, "People learn from observation, not conversation."

Check out your systems and procedures. Are they customer friendly? Do you make it difficult for the customer to do business with you? Are your forms easy to fill out, and are the procedures to buy from you the most efficient for the customer? What happens when a customer has a complaint? Have you made it easy to complain? All these things contribute to establishing a culture of service.

Have everyone from the top to the bottom ask, "What would the customer think? Would this make their experience easier? More convenient? More enjoyable?" With this thinking, the entire organization is constantly focused on the customer, and a deep awareness of a culture of service takes root.

Tom Rieger and Guido M.J. de Koning of The Gallup Organization say, "For a company to truly put customers first, it must focus all its processes, systems, infrastructure, policies and practices on that goal. The problem is, too many organizations are structured in ways that hinder achieving world-class levels of customer service."

These are just a few examples of how to help everyone see the vision of outstanding service in actual practice and how it affects their jobs. Only when this happens will you be on the road to establishing a true customer service culture.

Step Number Two: Develop a Service Vision or Target.

Aside from modeling behavior and making sure that all procedures and systems are for the customers' convenience, what else needs to be in place in order to create a culture of service? How do you go about creating a culture of service where, even if you aren't looking over everyone's shoulders, excellent customer service still happens?

- **Create a vision of what excellent customer service looks like and help each employee see how they can make it happen in their job.** Without a shared vision of what you mean by outstanding customer service, it can't happen. When you share your vision of what customer service should be, or have your employees help develop it, your employees will be able to act on their own. They will understand the level of commitment to customers that you support.

- An owner of a group of nursing and assisted living facilities roams the hall armed with a pocket of silver dollars. Any employee who can recite the company customer service vision and how they make it happen gets rewarded with a silver dollar.

- A customer service vision statement of a small retail store states: "We want our customers to view us as providing more than just acceptable service. Our goal is to provide legendary service in every shopping experience." Then each employee determines how they can provide legendary service in his or her job.

A vision is important for three reasons:

1. **A vision clarifies the direction that the company is taking.** It says, "This is where we are going, and everything and everybody should help make this happen." When everyone knows the direction in which you are headed, a common culture develops.

   A hospital has this vision: "Our competent and friendly team works together efficiently to create an environment in which our patients are confident in their medical care and assured of our concern for them and their health." Then they took each word and turned it into behaviors. For example, what did "friendly" look like? They determined that greeting every patient whenever they encountered them was part of that equation. "Competent" meant that everyone was fully trained in the latest medical knowledge and held current certifications.

2. **A vision helps people move out of their comfort zone.** New ways of doing things in order to achieve outstanding service will require people to do things differently.

   Cary Anderson, when he was CEO of Cosden Federal Credit Union in Big Spring, Texas, gave his tellers the new title of "service consultants." Their previous title was "tellers." But now they were responsible for knowing much more about their products and the benefits of each. Their new role was a lot different from the simple order takers and money dispensers that they were before. And it required that they do some things differently.

Anderson has always had a strong vision of what he wants superior member service to look like, and in his current CEO position at LA DOTD Federal Credit Union, he is constantly reminding everyone of this vision and is working to expand employees' comfort zones to get there.

3. **A vision helps to coordinate action.** If everybody knows exactly where you are headed, it will be much easier to get there. Employees can make decisions and take action without constantly checking with their boss or peers. Without a shared sense of vision, people will be unsure of what action to take.

Think of a typical situation in a grocery store when you ask a clerk who is busily stocking the shelves, "Where is the soup?" Does he grunt and point and say, "Two aisles over." Does he stop what he is doing and take you there? Does he know that you are more important than getting the shelves stocked? Does he have a smile on his face that says, "I remember that you are my paycheck and my most important priority," not, "You are an interruption in my day"? That's when your culture of service runs deep.

Here's another example. Today's banks are not known for being terribly customer friendly to the masses. It often seems that waiting in line is your main activity in a bank. A businessman who had been to the bank and several other places one day discovered that his keys were missing. In retracing his steps, he stopped back at the bank and inquired at the teller line if any keys had been found. Unfortunately, they were not found, but the teller asked for his card and said she'd call if they turned up.

A day later he found the keys and that was the end of the story—but it wasn't. Five days later, the teller called him to tell him that she was sorry, but they hadn't found the keys. Our businessman was flabbergasted that the bank teller had done this on her own. He told everyone he knew, spreading the kind of PR about the bank's service you can't buy. He even called the teller's boss to tell her what a great employee she had!

Because the bank had a strong vision of the kind of service they wanted to deliver, the teller understood that she should and could take the time to go the extra mile with that customer. No manager had to suggest it; she knew what to do because of the strong vision of service instilled by the bank.

- A small industrial supplier uses the following service vision: "We delight our customers with high-quality service, flexibility, responsiveness and quality relationships with customers that create value and opportunity." Employees now know what things are important in their delivery of service.

- An office supply firm that has successfully competed against the "big box" office supply stores uses exceptional customer service and an out-of-the-ordinary product selection to differentiate the company. Their vision statement simply says: "Our customers are everything!" Employees are empowered to bend over backwards to make whatever the customer wants happen.

Once you have established your vision, you must reinforce it regularly and involve employees in deciding how it will happen. Before you decide on a new customer form, for instance, ask both employees and customers if it is easy to understand and thus customer friendly.

You can't simply introduce your vision and expect people to buy into it immediately. It must be repeated again and again:

- Post it on the walls

- Start each meeting with the vision

- Print it on posters and mugs

- Display it in the employee break room

- Publish "hero" stories of good customer service examples that exemplify the vision in the customer newsletter

- Create a customer service vision "Hall of Fame" with employees' pictures

An owner of a small business has a meeting once a week with his shift leaders and stresses, "We are here to serve our customers." Every meeting reinforces that theme so that the vision is constantly in front of his employees.

Step Number Three: Constantly Check on the Level of Service Your Organization Is Delivering and Keep the Results in Front of Your Employees.

Continually measure your level of service so that it stays fresh in everyone's minds. Look at all aspects of your customers' experience to monitor your service culture. Make every employee aware of your report card.

Drury Inns often has their properties mystery shopped to test the level of service. When the ratings are high, the results are posted in the employee break room for everyone to see. When they don't measure up to expectations, employees or groups of employees responsible for the breakdown are privately coached to see what behaviors need to be changed.

Try experiencing some of your service points yourself. Not only will you gain valuable information on the level of service you are offering, but you will also send a powerful message to your employees about where customer service is on your priority list.

For example:

Have you ever tried to return something to your own business or had someone do this for you? Did you learn something that surprised you? Perhaps every one of your customers—and former customers—already knew this. The important point is that you are now in a position to make a change.

It's usually a lot harder to bring something back than to buy it. Few shoppers will deny that. But why? Many stores make it difficult to return something either by not having enough people to deal with returns, making the rules and procedures difficult to comply with, or being downright nasty about it. This sends a strong message to employees that the customer does not come first, regardless of what the vision states. Yet many of these store owners believe they are offering competitive-edge service, totally overlooking their "customer unfriendly" return policies. If you are guilty of this, you are merely paying lip service to advertised customer service. Remember, angry customers, because of a single incident at the Returns Department, quickly become former customers.

There are many possible solutions to this problem, such as having the right person in place or a streamlined procedure. Or better yet, if you are in a retail environment, you can turn it to your advantage with a "drop-off" return desk that will turn the credit around in 15 minutes and suggesting that the customer shop while they wait.

Another way to check your level of service is to call your place of business to see how your phone system is working. Is your automated routing system too hard to navigate? Were you tempted to hang up and take your business elsewhere? Did you find poor service or some version of "voice mail hell?" I'm not surprised.

Like many others, Sue Burnett, President of Burnett Staffing Specialists, hates when there are too many choices in an automated system. In general, she doesn't like her phone answered by a machine, and finds it particularly annoying when she has to punch in someone's name when she doesn't know their extension number. "And sometimes you don't know anyone's name in the company," she says.

Burnett also hates excessive "over screening." "That's when they question you extensively," she notes. "I don't have anyone screen anything to anyone in my company; I think it is poor customer service." She has been in business for 30 years and has never had her calls screened.

You have to wonder—do companies purposely make it as difficult as they can to keep the customer from reaching a real person? The truth is that often their focus is on saving money by hiring fewer employees rather than serving their customers and making the company easy to do business with.

When you are informed and care about how your customers are being treated, you will be able to stop your customers from leaving and going down the street to your competitors. You will also have "walked your talk" about the importance of customer service. After all, if you care enough to check on the level of service, it will send a strong message to your employees that service is indeed important.

Whether you are a medical practice, retail store, government entity, franchise, service provider, manufacturing organization or one of many other kinds of businesses, you need to keep tabs on what your customer is experiencing by way of service. Chapter Three outlines more ways to keep abreast of the level of customer satisfaction in your organization.

Step Number Four: Create a Climate of Celebration

Creating a celebratory atmosphere when your company receives good customer service feedback is critical to developing a culture of service. How can you do this? Notice when your employees are doing it right and celebrate it. Reward them in some small way so as to encourage this behavior.

Celebrate everything:

- When a customer writes a letter or gives verbal praise about the level of service they received

- When a customer service comment card comes back with a high rating for service

- When employees have gone the extra mile to serve a customer

- When mystery shopping reports are good

- When you or a manager observes an employee delivering exceptional customer service

Theresa Casa, President of Casa's Catering Company, knows that having fun is an important part of dealing with the heavy stress of her business. Whenever her crew has just finished a big project and done well, she gives each of them a "clapper hand." Those are toy hands that clap themselves together. She says, "I want you to give yourself a hand" as she passes them out. Everyone has a good laugh and feels appreciated.

Chapter Ten provides more ideas on ways to celebrate and reward exceptional service behavior, so your employees deliver superior customer service to every customer, every time.

Step Number Five: Customer Service Training Must Always Be Customized for Your Business.

Any program you develop or secure from an outside consultant cannot be a generic, one-size-fits-all program. "Training in a box" cannot result in a superior customer service program. You can use this book to help you develop your own specific approach even if you work in partnership with a consultant or use a generic training program as your base.

Sometimes you can supplement your program with videotapes or customer service newsletters or books; however, the main core of the program must come from you and be specifically tailored to your environment.

After all, only you know the delicate politics of the company and how to go about selling the idea of superior service to your employees. You know the hot buttons. You know that service issues will be somewhat different in a credit union than in a bank. You will know how much time will be appropriate for training sessions and how best to communicate with your employees. For instance, can one of your communication channels be e-mail or learning via computer? Or would your people prefer face-to-face meetings?

A good example of an organization creating a culture of service by using many of the steps listed above is United Space Alliance, LLC. Mark White, Director of Procurement and Strategic Sourcing, says, "You don't have to be in the retail business to use the delivery of superior customer service to your advantage." Their vision in his department is "We want to be world class," and everything is pointed toward that.

They use a customer service survey each year and many other metrics and benchmarks to measure their success. Some of these include:

- How quickly, on average, the buyers complete requisitions and purchase orders

- How well their expediting process meets the customers' needs

- The quality of the materials that originally appear on the United Space Alliance receiving docks

- The response time to clear any discrepancy with the parts and materials upon receipt

White is also well known for his "Markisms" that help reinforce the importance of superior service to their customers—other employees and NASA.

Some examples:

- Never tell a customer: "It's not my job." Take five minutes to find the right person to help the customer.

- People do business with people, not companies, systems or computers.

- Never talk bad about your customers; it always gets back to you.

- Periodically ask your customers how you are doing.

- Don't blame the process, explain the process.

- Never blame an internal department for a delay.

White also has a list of things that each manager should do to help plant the culture of service.

- Make sure employees know that customer service is part of their job and part of their performance evaluation.

- Make sure you or your employees attend the right customer service meetings.

- Go visit your customers periodically, even if it costs money.

- Customer service training has to be looked at as another tool to get the job done.

- On-the-spot awards or management acknowledgement should be given to employees in every instance when customers make it a point to communicate a good service incident about one of your employees.

- Develop a strong set of metrics that measure your performance and communicate how well you are doing for your customers.

If your organization truly has a culture of service, every action is pointed toward the customer. Everybody in the organization must understand that it is everyone's job to take care of the customer. It must be the driving force of the business and each employee must be constantly aware that, "The customer is our paycheck—no customers, no paycheck." In this way, you get extraordinary service behaviors from your employees.

A truly service-driven company is also totally committed to supporting employees in their efforts to deliver competitive-edge service. In such a company, they not only give employees the right to make decisions, but they also give them the freedom to break the rules when the rules get in the way.

Another important component of developing a culture of service is to treat your suppliers like customers. In most businesses, you can't deliver competitive-edge service without the cooperation of outstanding suppliers. Establish a supplier-recognition program to encourage suppliers to give you the kind of service that will enable you to serve your customers well.

Self Test: Do You Have a Culture of Service?

Here are more elements that create a culture of service that will be discussed in the book. How do you rate? Rank each statement "always", "sometimes" or "never."

1. We continually monitor our customers' expectations of service so we can adjust our service to those levels of expectations.
    ____**Always** ____**Sometimes** ____**Never**

2. We have a regular customer feedback system in place. It is more than one method: e.g., customer comment cards, customer panels, telephone surveys, one-on-one feedback, etc.
    ____**Always** ____**Sometimes** ____**Never**

3. We use this feedback to improve our processes and the way our employees deliver service. It does not just sit on a desk somewhere.
    ____**Always** ____**Sometimes** ____**Never**

4. We have a service vision that is short, memorable and employees can state how they individually make the vision come alive.
    ____**Always** ____**Sometimes** ____**Never**

5. We look at each customer contact point to make sure it is a positive experience.
    ____**Always** ____**Sometimes** ____**Never**

6. We evaluate all our policies and procedures to make sure they are customer friendly and do not make it hard to do business with us.
    ____**Always** ____**Sometimes** ____**Never**

7. We use our interviewing process to make sure we hire applicants who are customer-focused and have the skills to deliver excellent customer service.
    ____**Always** ____**Sometimes** ____**Never**

8. Our orientation program stresses the importance of delivering excellent customer service.
    ____**Always** ____**Sometimes** ____**Never**

9. We train and retrain all levels of our employees, including upper management, in both technical and customer service skills. The training is tailored to the level of the employee.
    ____**Always** ____**Sometimes** ____**Never**

10. Employees' performance appraisals contain a section on the delivery of superior customer service.
    ____Always ____Sometimes ____Never

11. Compensation of all employees is based partially on the achievement of outstanding customer service, both in the individual department and the company as a whole.
    ____Always ____Sometimes ____Never

12. Managers and supervisors model the best service skills at all times.
    ____Always ____Sometimes ____Never

13. The company owners or high-level executives spend time with customers to get their views of the level of service being delivered.
    ____Always ____Sometimes ____Never

14. We hold regular staff meetings to talk about the importance of customer service and to get input from the customer service front line.
    ____Always ____Sometimes ____Never

Scoring

Give yourself 2 points for every "Always," 1 point for every "Sometimes," and 0 points for every "Never." Then rate yourself.

42-36 = Keep it up, you are well on the way to establishing a strong culture of service.

35-29 = Reread this chapter to determine in what areas you can improve.

Below 29 = You have a lot of work to do toward establishing a culture of service. Sit down and make a plan now.

So how did you do? If you weren't happy with your score, read on. As you can tell from the test above, a comprehensive program for customer service does not consist of simply putting your employees through a training course, or declaring in a team retreat that the customer is number one. It must begin with planting a culture of service and devising a careful plan. Each of the elements mentioned above will be covered more fully in the following chapters.

CHAPTER THREE

How to Solicit Customer Opinions of Your Service

Everything flows from the voice of your customer. You **must get** customer feedback on a regular basis or you will never understand what your customers find valuable and what they want in the way of service. Without a **direct line** of feedback, you can never hope to offer the kind of outstanding service that will give you the competitive-edge.

• Everything must flow from what the customer wants and values

• Learning your customers' expectations and then exceeding them is critical to outdistancing your competition

You cannot rely on intuition when determining customers' expectations and opinions of actual service. At this level, you are only guessing at the desires and wishes of your customers. For example, you may think that your customers are happy with a response time of 24 hours when they are really expecting 12 or 2 hours!

Don't be afraid to ask your customers what they want. You will not have to "give away the store." Most customer desires are very reasonable. It is only when they don't receive what they perceive to be good service that they get ugly and make unreasonable demands. Remember, all their ideas are worth considering. You may not agree with them and you may not use them all, but there is always something to be learned.

Once you have discovered those expectations, you must also constantly measure how you are doing relative to those expectations. When you monitor how you are doing on a regular basis, your customers will tell you what you are doing right as well as what you are doing wrong.

Ways to Obtain Customer Feedback

You can do the same thing that the NFL Houston Texans do, only on a smaller level. This chapter will tell you how.

There are three basic things you must learn from your customers to build or maintain a high level of service:

1. What service characteristics matter the most to them?

2. How well are you doing in delivering the service?

3. What do they find to be wrong or missing?

Getting the answers is often not simple because people may not be forthcoming, don't have time or—worst of all—know they will never come back after a negative experience. Customer feedback involves listening to your customers through various channels and using as many of them as you possibly can. As a manager, it is important to be involved directly in this feedback loop. If you use just one method, your results will not be as accurate.

The NFL Houston Texans football team is aware of the importance of getting customer feedback. Before their inaugural season, they held a series of customer panels to discuss fans' game day expectations so they could plan to make it happen. Next, they sent Internet evaluations after each game, conducted mystery shopping and held a series of new customer panels to determine how well they were doing in meeting those fan expectations.

The basic channels that everyone must use:

1. **Make it a point to personally call or visit a cross section of your customers.**

If you don't naturally interface with your customers every day, make some time to do so. Visit your customers at their place of business or take them to lunch or dinner or an entertainment or sporting event. Pump them for information on what they like and don't like about your service. As a small or medium size business, you can do this, and the customer will be very impressed that you are taking the time to do this personally.

Ask them what they think about the level of service you are currently delivering, and ask questions like, "If there is one thing about our product or service you could change, what would it be?"

Do not ask, "How is our service?" That will result in the "fine" response. They will tell you that everything is fine when it actually isn't.

You've seen examples of this. At a restaurant, a table of diners bitterly complain about the food and the service. Yet when the waiter arrives and asks, "How is everything?" they all turn and say, "Fine." When the waiter leaves, they quickly start complaining again. The restaurant employees falsely believe they are doing a good job, when in reality they are not. How many of your customers have just quietly gone away when you thought everything was fine?

2. Be sure to conduct exit interviews with customers who leave without making a purchase or are clearly unhappy.

Find out why they are leaving, and don't accept price as the only answer. If they use price, they usually mean you are not providing enough value for them. Value, as discussed in Chapter One, is the combination of things and experiences that create a perception of getting your money's worth. If the perception is not positive, your customers will not believe they are receiving enough value. Sometimes you can win customers back when you discover a problem and fix it.

Here's a story of how a negative customer reaction can be turned around. A couple was eating in a very popular and hectic neighborhood pizza restaurant where they eat virtually every week. The establishment was family owned, always busy and had good service. The night of this incident was similar to other nights, except for one thing—the service seemed to be slower than usual. After about 15 minutes of waiting, when the waitress walked by, the couple said to her, "We're ready to order now."

Instead of stopping or acknowledging them, she turned and said, "You know you aren't the only ones here!" Of course, they were shocked speechless. Within a minute, the couple decided that leaving was the best option. However, as they walked out, one stopped and told the manager/owner what had happened. To avoid further unpleasantness, they quickly left.

Sound familiar? You have probably heard this story many, many times. Usually both parties lose, but not in this case.

A month later, the couple decided to go back to the restaurant—they missed the pizza! They sat down at an empty table, and within a couple of minutes the owner was at their table. Not only did he apologize for the incident and indicate that he had reprimanded the waitress, but he also gave them their pizza free. "I am so sorry," he said, "I thought I'd lost you." And that was the perfect thing to say. Not only was the couple shocked that he'd remembered them, but now they felt the owner of this little pizza parlor valued their business. This is how you make a customer for life. And it could only have happened with the owner listening to his customer's feedback.

Here's another example of how an unhappy customer's feedback could have proven useful. A very successful dermatologist's office recently received a call from a long-term patient asking for her records. Without asking why, the office took down the mailing information and complied.

Our patient was quite disappointed. First, no one seemed to care that she was leaving, and second, no one even asked why. Actually she liked the doctor and her treatment results had been positive.

In truth, the patient was leaving because the doctor pushed his skin care products and this made her feel uncomfortable. She was leaving for that reason and that reason only. Would that be valuable information for the doctor? You bet! If one patient feels this way, you can be assured that others do, too, and someday may be preparing to leave.

Medical practices are a model of a "small" business with major customer contact. Practitioners should be aware of customer feedback, especially in this day of managed care and reduced patient options due to insurance. But many do not spend the time or effort to find out how their patients perceive them.

3. Contact your competitors' customers.

This is a no-brainer, yet many people are reluctant to do this. Perhaps they are afraid of their competitors doing this to them. It's likely they already have, and given most people's reluctance to volunteer information, this may be your best chance of learning about your own deficiencies.

Ask why they are not buying from you. Is it your service or your price? Or is it some other aspect of customer value that we discussed before? This will result in a goldmine of information. It will help you make your product and service more attractive to potential customers. It will also illustrate how your competitors are exceeding expectations for your kind of product or service. Professionals rarely put this idea to use, but they should.

One attorney in a small law firm described his technique for uncovering information. Over the years, he made it a habit to ask virtually everyone he met which law firm they used and what they liked about their service. He was able to learn several ways that his firm could offer something extra in order to exceed his customers' expectations and, not surprisingly, it was the "little things" that made the difference.

For instance, he learned that prompt returns of phone calls (what a surprise!!!) were critical in a client's perception of whether he received good or bad service. And that "prompt" meant within two hours. So his firm set a service target of returning all phone calls within one hour in order to exceed those expectations. If the attorney was unavailable or in court, someone else from the firm returned the call and made careful notes so the caller didn't have to repeat his request multiple times.

Most likely, you will learn what you already know, like the phone call return issue. However, hearing it directly from a competitor's customer is very motivating and can be a powerful force of change in your own company.

4. Listen and ask for "I wish" statements.

"I wish you had music in the birthday rooms," said the customer. "My child has some favorite tunes I would like to play during her birthday party." The business owner listened to that statement and put CD players in the birthday rooms so the customer could have what she wanted. It has proved to be a popular feature of their birthday celebrations—one that sets them just a little bit apart and makes the customer feel special.

If you really listen, customers will often say things like:

- I wish you were open in the evenings. It would be much more convenient for me.

- If only you offered a pocketed t-shirt.

- I wish I could do this online. XYZ Company does it; why can't you?

As mentioned in Chapter One, "I wish" statements will tell you what your customers value and will pay money for.

Actively probe for customers' wishes. Ask questions like:

"What do you wish we did differently?"

"Can you think of any product or service that you wish we would add?"

These statements will usually fall into one of three categories: emerging trends; opportunities for service improvement; or new ideas for products and services. Make a list of these wishes and share this list with employees in a meeting. Then brainstorm ways that you can make these happen.

5. **Send something to your customers.**

This is a must and something that most businesses don't think of as feedback. Send birthday, Thanksgiving, holiday or Fourth of July cards. It doesn't matter what the occasion; just let them know you are thinking of them.

A piece of mail will often trigger a response from the customer about some unmet expectations or something you need to fix in order to keep them happy with your service. Reply to any correspondence they send you, even if it appears no response is required (e.g., a compliment about your service). Always send thank you notes to both new and regular customers or clients.

- A sprinkler company sends a thank you card after each service to stimulate a response from his customers. He receives both positive and negative calls from his customers. This enables him to see what he is doing right and to correct anything that did not meet the customer's expectations.

- A family-owned jewelry store located in an upscale suburb not only has competition in town but also from chain stores in at least three malls within a 20 minute drive. This is a common story today. Established businesses are fighting for customer share but yet can't always offer the same discounts as the big guys. However, they can differentiate themselves by soliciting and acting on customer feedback.

The local jeweler collects information on its customers—especially the reason for a purchase, like an engagement ring—and follows up with a handwritten note announcing sales and mentioning some ideas for presents at birthday time. The customer feels special, and at the same time, the store is promoting their service, differentiating themselves and staying in touch with their customers.

This customer is more likely to take the time to give feedback on positives and negatives to the store owners. This lets them know what to keep doing more of and what needs to be changed in order to help them stand out from the chain stores.

6. **Make sure it is easy for your customers to contact you and there is a mechanism in place to respond.**

Although it adds some cost, having a toll-free telephone number makes customers more likely to let you know when their expectations are not being met. This provides you with the chance to make it right.

A customer was unhappy with the quality of the Oscar Meyer bacon he just bought; it was fatty with very little meat. Vowing never to buy any more of that brand, frustrated and not willing to take the time to return it to the grocery store, he noticed an 800 number on the package.

Picking up the phone, he easily (didn't have to go through ten choices to reach a real person) reached a friendly customer service representative who assured him they were sincerely happy for his call. They wanted to know when something was wrong with the product. She went on to say that she would send him coupons good for two free packages of bacon.

Would this customer have complained if the company did not have an 800 number? Probably not. The company would never have known they were losing customers due to poor quality. Because of this positive resolution, he is still a customer of Oscar Meyer and buys other products made by that company.

To prevent your customers from going to your competitors, you should have a button on your Web home page that enables customers to reach you with the click of a button. Have an auto responder on your Web site, if possible, to let your customers know that you have received their request. Tell them you will reply within 24 hours or some other time frame. Then make sure you have someone to respond to those e-mails within the promised time period.

Avoid sending back a form response with no personalization. Since you are a small or medium size business, you can make yourself stand out from the big guys by personalizing the e-mail reply.

7. **Take a "How Are We Doing" survey of your customers whenever the opportunity presents itself.**

Be fanatic about listening to what your customers want and value, rather than **assuming you know what they want and then delivering only that. Use frequent surveys to listen to your customers.**

Some examples:

- Diagnostic Imaging Services, a medical imaging firm based in New Orleans, Louisiana, is very proactive in their patient feedback methods. As each patient leaves, they are given a postage paid survey form.

The surveys are reviewed daily. All patient comments are acknowledged by Gina Curtis, Director of Marketing. If it is a positive comment, she writes a note thanking them; if it is negative, Curtis personally calls them to find out more. The underlying cause of the problem—whether it be a person or a procedure—is investigated to see that it does not happen again.

The imaging technician, who actually performs the procedure, asks at the end of the appointment, "Is there anything about your visit that we need to know about?" The overwhelming response is positive, but if they get a negative comment, it is immediately dealt with by a manager or Curtis.

She also visits referring physicians' offices to get to know them better. This way they will feel more comfortable telling her when things are not to their satisfaction.

- Most hotels, fine restaurants and other businesses, where a wide variety of employees come in contact with a customer, use this method to get ongoing feedback. A hotel, for example, can have one of the finest restaurants in town or the best bar, but if the maids don't clean the bathroom well or the front desk doesn't pick up promptly, the visitor will find a new hotel—probably the one across the street! You find out about the break-downs from constant feedback.

- The Hyatt Regency Hotel in downtown Houston takes every opportunity to get feedback from their guests. They even have the valet parkers asking guests for feedback on their stays.

- Kohl's Department Stores print their Web site and an 800 number on every receipt along with the phrase, "Give us your feedback on today's store visit," in case the customer has a comment, good or bad.

- Don't be afraid to be innovative in the way you get feedback. A car repair company sends their customers home in a prepaid taxi and pays the taxi drivers to relate any comments the passengers make about the level of service they just received. The drivers gently pump their passengers for information and pass it on to the car repair company.

Comprehensive Questionnaires and Surveys Can Be Valuable But...

Make questionnaires and surveys short, easy-to-answer and offer some reward for doing it. They can be mailed, faxed, e-mailed or given to the customer at the point of contact. Limit the number of fill-in-the-blank questions; you will increase your response rate.

- Danny O'Daniels, owner of O'Daniels Garage, mails a questionnaire to about 3,000 customers two or three times a year, asking questions like: "How can we do better at our service?" "Are we friendly enough?" "How is our front office staff?" and others. He gets an astonishing return of about 2,200 to 2,600 cards by offering a small discount on one of his services if they return the card.

- A restaurant has initiated an aggressive program to solicit customer feedback through the use of customer comment cards. One employee (on a rotating basis) is assigned the task of personally asking guests at each table to fill out a feedback card. If they agree, the card is left at the table with a pen. Guests deposit the cards in a box at the front door as they exit. They are also given a coupon good for a free appetizer the next time they visit. This is smart! It not only encourages customers to fill out the comment card, but it also brings them back to spend more money.

Here are some possible questions to ask:

- What are we doing well?

- What are we NOT doing well?

- What are we NOT doing that we should be doing?

- What are we doing that we should NOT be doing?

- What would make you feel you had really received value for your money?

- If you could change just one thing about our service, what would it be?

- If this were your company and your money, what would you change?

- Has our service gone up or down in the last six months?

- How can we change the way we provide products or services to you to make life easier for you?

Some sample questionnaires

From a city...

	Strongly Agree	Agree	Disagree	Strongly Disagree
The staff treated me courteously and professionally.				
Service was provided in a timely manner.				
Overall I am delighted with the service I received.				
My questions were answered or problems solved.				

If not, how could we solve your problems?

_____

_____

If a member of our staff provided you with especially outstanding service, please let us know his or her name:

_____

An automobile repair shop

Circle the most appropriate rating:

	Poor							Excellent		
Your expectations were met	1	2	3	4	5	6	7	8	9	10
Staff knowledgeable, courteous and efficient	1	2	3	4	5	6	7	8	9	10
Vehicle ready when promised	1	2	3	4	5	6	7	8	9	10
Center clean and organized	1	2	3	4	5	6	7	8	9	10
Overall performance of staff	1	2	3	4	5	6	7	8	9	10

I was helped by:

_____

Comments:

_____

_____

How can we serve you better?

_____

_____

Thank you!

(Name of the owners)

In appreciation, your name will be entered in our quarterly prize drawing.

Name: _____

Phone: _____

Try to catch people's eyes by making yours different. For example you could paste a piece of candy to the feedback card with a statement like, "Treat us to your opinion!"

Suggestions of titles for your reply card

- If you don't have anything nice to say, say it anyway

- Help us give you the STAR treatment by filling out this card

- Grade Us!

- Help us help you

- Just between you and me…How was everything?

Other Ways to Gather Customer Feedback.

Focus groups

Gather a small group of your customers and ask them what they like about your product or service. Then ask them about any problems they are having and their expectations of what should happen when they do business with you. Keep the size down to 10-12 people for a period of no longer than two hours and give careful consideration to the group compensation.

You can usually pay focus group members a minimum of $25 and something to eat. Many of your customers will do it for free because they are flattered to be asked their opinions. Other times you can give them small gifts.

The NFL Houston Texans provided dinner for their customer focus groups and gave participants a gift of Texans logo merchandise.

Choose a representative sample of your customers across different age groups, ethnic backgrounds, income levels, etc. If possible, it is good to conduct more than one focus group, so you get opinions from as many customers as possible.

By the way, most product development companies and ad agencies use this technique, and you can, too, no matter what your business. A second similar method is a Mall Intercept that can be done very informally. Simply send someone to a local mall near your establishment and have them stop random people in your demographic category (e.g., women in their 30s for a clothing boutique, men of all ages for electronics). Ask questions to learn what they know about you. Do you have a good reputation for service? Are your employees knowledgeable about the products you sell? See if these answers support data from your focus groups.

Telephone surveys

Many of the same questions developed for your survey can be used in a script for a telephone calling survey. Be sure that the person doing the survey is well trained and can handle complaints well—and even take verbal abuse.

The main disadvantage of telephone surveys is that the respondent can hang up at any time, or may not even talk to you. Plus, people are busy and do not want to take time away from their personal lives to complete the survey.

But whatever you do, don't make the mistake of only using one method of obtaining customer feedback. Try to use at least two, and three if possible, in order to get an accurate picture of your customers' expectations and how well you are meeting those expectations.

Front-line employee encounters with the customer

Your employees are the ones who are in regular contact with the customers. As a result, they know a great deal about customers' expectations and perceptions. They hear the complaints and the "I wish" statements. They know where your systems are breaking down in the effort to service the customer. Develop a system where you can capture this information.

A veterinarian's office has a weekly meeting. All of the staff gathers together to discuss their customer interactions—both good and bad. Then they engage in a problem-solving session to eliminate the less-than-perfect service incidents. Other businesses use a suggestion box to capture their employees' ideas.

Face-to-face personal interviews

This is one of the simplest ways to assess customer satisfaction and to learn where you are not meeting their expectations. By asking what your customers like and don't like about your business, you can find your strengths and weaknesses.

Sohil Merchant, Managing Director of Knight Systems, a computer networking and software development firm, likes to use the personal touch. He feels that no one wants to sit down and take the time to fill out a survey anymore. So he takes his clients out to lunch, dinner or a round of golf. In this setting he works one-on-one with them to uncover his or her expectations and contentment with the company's service. He likes to ask questions like, "Is there anything we can do to make things better for you?"

In-house customer panels

Get five to seven of your customers on a panel in front of your employees. Let them talk about your service and what they like and don't like. There is nothing more powerful than hearing and seeing your customers talk about your service in person. Appendix B gives you detailed instructions on how to conduct an in-house customer panel.

Videotape Your Customers. The Results May Surprise You!

If it is difficult to get all your employees together in one place, perhaps you can videotape a group of several customers talking about what they like and don't like about your service. Then play it back for your employees.

Here's an assignment for you to help you get started in getting the customer feedback you need.

- List the top five reasons you think your customers buy from you.

- Determine your best customers.

- Take them to lunch or interview them, one at a time, and ask why they buy from you.

- Compare your list with your customers' responses.

So how are you doing at obtaining continual feedback from your customers? Determining your customers' expectations and getting feedback is a full-time job for everyone in the business. You don't do it just once a year, check it off the list and then move on to other things.

When you are continually monitoring your customers' satisfaction levels, it will help you identify new trends, develop new products and services and involve your customers in your business. It will also help you find out what you are doing wrong while letting your customers feel important and valuable. You also impress upon your customers your desire to constantly improve. Exceptional service starts by listening to your customers—then making sure every employee hears it.

How are you doing with customer feedback?

Check all that apply:

❑   We obtain customer feedback on a regular basis

❑   All employees, as well as top executives, are always involved in the feedback process

❑   We use at least three forms of feedback

❑   We conduct exit interviews with our customers who stop doing business with us, if possible

❑   The information is compiled within one week of receiving it

❑   Customers' negative feedback is acknowledged within 24 hours of receipt

❑   Letters replying to complaining customers are personalized

❑   Both positive and negative feedback are distributed to all staff and discussed in staff meetings if appropriate

❑   Employees' ideas are solicited on how to fix any problems unearthed by the feedback

Scoring:

7-9 checks = Congratulations. You are doing a good job in getting customer feedback. Keep it up.

4-6 checks = You are on the way to using customer feedback to create a level of service that will give you the competitive edge, but you need to incorporate more of the ideas in this chapter.

Less than 4 = You need to recognize that you will never be able to achieve a level of service that will give you the competitive-edge unless you start listening to your customers more. Use some of the suggestions in this chapter.

CHAPTER FOUR

Setting Service Targets

So far you have:

- Determined your service vision

- Taken steps to plant a culture of service that begins at the top

- Found out what your customer wants and expects from your service

- Discovered how you are doing on delivering it

Now it is time to set service targets or goals based on those expectations. These targets will help everyone understand exactly what behaviors are necessary in order for your customers to feel they are receiving excellent service.

Some companies call them "best practices," some call them "service standards," others "service targets or goals." In each case they are specific, easily understood goals for the level of service to be delivered and the behaviors needed to reach those goals. It helps to show employees the goals expected in each part of their job.

Remember: you can't just tell employees to "give excellent service." You must specifically define exactly what "excellent service" means in behavioral terms.

What should they do or not do?

What should they say or not say?

If employees are to serve your customers in a consistent fashion, they must clearly understand what excellent service looks like based on customer expectations.

Consider the drugstore chain that simplified the service experience to four behaviors:

1. Smile, look the customer in the eyes and greet the customer as soon as you see them approach.

2. If they look lost or are looking for something, ask how you can help them.

3. Take them to where they can find what they want.

4. Say "good-bye" to the customer as they leave. Add, "Thanks for coming in."

The customer satisfaction ratings of the drugstore went up from an "average" to an "outstanding" score as a result of following these simple behaviors, performed for every customer, every time.

When you are specific about what you expect regarding service behaviors, you make your employees accountable and responsible for their actions. Your employees understand very clearly what customers want and how they should deliver it. It makes them accountable for their behaviors, whether the boss is looking or not.

In addition, you will need some discretionary behaviors to avoid turning your employees into robots. That's why planting a *culture* of service focusing on the customer is so important. But employees, especially in a high turnover situation, must begin with specific behaviors.

You must bring new employees on board very quickly and service goals will help them understand from the first exactly what behaviors are expected. They should be included in your orientation program and reinforced often during the first days on the job.

Putt-Putt FunHouse based in Houston, Texas, hires "Party Entertainers" who organize and entertain at birthday parties. During the tryout for the job, employees are told they will be evaluated on the following job criteria:

- Consistently perform in innovative ways to surprise, go beyond expectations and "Wow" party parents.

- Always maintain high levels of energy, smiles and enthusiasm. Actively interact with children at "their level" throughout the entire two-hour party.

- Stay with the party child and guests, while always remaining available and checking in with the party mom to ensure needs are met and that she knows we care.

- Pre-call, greet, organize play, serve food and facilitate the celebration of all

Putt-Putt Funhouse's party components and activities in a timely manner and within the time period scheduled.

- Make sure the birthday child is the center of attention at each party you host.

- Be a team player and be willing to help others when needed.

- Maintain your party magic and entertainment kit. You must always be prepared, keep entertainment options fresh and replace any props or materials needed to perform.

Setting goals or targets and then having your employees accomplish them also develops pride in your employees through their service delivery. People know when they have done a good job and feel good about themselves and their work. When you hit your service goals consistently, customers and employees alike benefit.

How to Develop Service Targets

So how do you go about developing specific service goals or targets and the behaviors that make them happen at your company?

First, if possible, start with getting your employees involved in the process; don't just impose the targets on them. They will appreciate it and will exhibit more "buy in" and less resentment. When people have a hand in determining what goes on, they will be much more enthusiastic about it and live up to the targets. This will always reinforce employee loyalty. If the service targets are already established, ask your employees how they could be improved or tweaked.

Keep in mind that setting service goals this way takes time, but it will pay off in achieving the kind of service, consistently, that will make you more profitable and gain you the reputation that your company delivers exceptional service and therefore gives value to their customers.

It takes time to think through how your team should behave in different service situations. It takes time to involve your employees in the decision process. It takes time to find out from your customers if your standards are on target.

What happens if you don't take this time? Inconsistent service happens. Some employees will deliver excellent service some of the time; others won't. Then you will have to spend your time coaching the employees who don't do it right and dealing with upset customers. Doesn't it make more sense to spend your time ensuring that your employees get it right the first time?

Some Simple Steps in This Process

- Start with making a list of each moment of contact the customer has with your company—customer touch points—and what your customers expect at each point of their experience with you. For instance, when a customer approaches your place of business, what happens first? Is she greeted within 30 seconds with a smile? If the employee is busy with other customers, does she at least acknowledge the customer with a statement like, "I'll be with you shortly."

What happens next? Are they passed to another employee? How is the customer touched at that point? Continue this process until you have listed every point of contact with the customer.

Using the information from your customer feedback, develop basic service targets based on what your customers want most from your service. Concentrate on the things that your customers have told you were most important to them.

Also keep in mind what your competitors are doing. Where are they most vulnerable? What can you do that your competitors can't? For instance, can you respond to a service request faster? Can you offer home delivery?

Next, you need to set up your systems to make it possible for your employees to reach these targets. There is nothing more frustrating for a customer service representative than to be told to answer the phone by the third ring but then find it impossible due to the volume of incoming calls and short staffing.

Continue going through each point of contact and, based on what you have found your customers expect, determine the specific, realistic behaviors that will make those expectations happen. If they are not realistic, you will find that employees will quickly discard the goals and go back to doing whatever is comfortable for them.

A list of service goals for the front desk at a large medical clinic contains the following:

- Stand up when the patient approaches and greet them with "hello," a smile and direct eye contact.

- Make sure your name badge is visible and easily read.

- Ask how you may help them in a warm and friendly manner.

Example: "May I please have your insurance card?" Not, "Where's your insurance card?"

- Tell them the approximate time it will take to be served. Always underestimate and over deliver. That means if you think it will take 30 minutes, tell them 35, so they will be surprised and delighted when it takes less time.

- Thank them and use their name. Be sure to pronounce it correctly.

- If they have already had a bad experience, (no parking, couldn't find their way, sent to the wrong place, etc) go out of your way to overwhelm them with good service. Do what you can to either fix the situation or to apologize for it. (Even if it wasn't your fault!)

When setting service targets, ensure that employees will have the latitude to do whatever is necessary to please the customer and that the targets do not conflict with each other. For example, expecting workers to be warm and friendly when serving the customer while also insisting that they adhere to a rigid time constraint will just result in frustrated customer service representatives who don't know which target to honor.

Call centers of all kinds, doctors' offices, and technology help lines often make this mistake. They measure the length of the calls and therefore make the customer service representative feel rushed. Try instead to measure customer satisfaction by using the customer service feedback techniques discussed in the previous chapter. Calls can be tape recorded and the customer service representatives graded on their achievement of the service targets.

Also be sure that your service targets include a clear plan for dealing with unhappy customers. It is particularly important to be clear about protocol in this area. It will help your employees deal with irate customers more effectively and prevent loss of business. In addition to behaviors like apologizing for the inconvenience even if the customer is at fault, define a list of recovery options. For example, offer a 10 percent discount on their next order or offer overnight delivery of replacement parts. The next chapter will deal more fully with this issue.

One last point: Beware of too many service targets or goals. You need to boil the targets down to the actions that your customers value most. Do just enough targets so employees can easily remember them. You should have no more than six service targets.

A small gym and fitness center has just four service standards for the front desk:

1. Customers will be greeted immediately and pleasantly.

2. Ask for their member number, enter it into the system and offer them a towel.

3. Keep personal conversations, food and telephone calls out of sight and hearing of customers.

4. Acknowledge them as they leave.

Remember:

- Keep the targets alive. If they are recorded in a manual that's collecting dust on a shelf somewhere, they are likely to be quickly forgotten. Keep your targets short and simple to remember and post them where every employee can see them every day. A short reminder card or other form of job aid also works well, so employees can quickly refer to it when they have questions. Have your employees review it in staff meetings to remind them of the specific service targets everyone should deliver to every customer, every time.

When the Houston Astros baseball team opened their new ballpark, they made sure that every employee dealing with the fans had a reminder card in their back pocket to help them remember the customer service targets.

- Revisit the goals often to evaluate how things are going and whether revisions are in order. Customers' expectations are constantly changing and your service targets need to reflect that.

Checklist for Developing Service Targets

Follow this checklist when you develop and evaluate your service targets.

❏ Are the targets clear and easy to understand for everyone involved?

❏ Do you have a method of keeping the targets in front of everyone on a regular basis?

❏ Can the targets be easily observed and measured?

❏ Are employees evaluated and rewarded on the targets on a regular basis?

❏ Can most of your employees achieve the targets?

❏ Were they developed by a team of employees and their managers?

❏ Do you re-evaluate the targets on a regular basis?

❏ Do you check your systems to make sure they enable the targets to happen?

❏ Do you have a feedback system to help judge when a target is unrealistic?

❏ Do you have a disciplinary action for when targets aren't met?

Scoring:

9–10 checks = Excellent. You are using service targets well.

6–8 checks = You have the right idea, but if your service targets are to be used successfully, you must institute some of the changes discussed in this chapter.

5 checks or below = You have some work to do on your service targets. Get going!

Remember: when your whole team is clear about what they should do and are measured and rewarded, you have taken the next step toward creating impressive customer service. This is the kind of customer service that brings your customers back again and again while referring others.

CHAPTER FIVE

The Importance of Complaining Customers

Customer complaints are a key to customer service AND more profits!

Do you ever have to deal with angry, unhappy customers? Of course you do.

You're in business aren't you? But how do you view customer complaints? As a pain and something to be avoided at all costs? Or as an opportunity to learn how to make your business even more attractive to your customers?

The way that you deal with those unhappy customers will have a critical impact on your business. After all, no business or organization can please all their customers all the time. Things will go wrong. Importantly, the way you handle those complaining customers makes all the difference in whether or not they return to do business with you again. If you get it wrong, they may generate bad word-of-mouth advertising that hurts your business. If you get it right, they may turn into cheerleaders for your business.

Service mishaps can directly affect your company's profits. Technical Assistance Research Programs (TARP) cites this research:

- After they experience a problem, customer's loyalty drops an average of 20%

- For each five customers with a problem, one will be placed at risk

The way you deal with every unhappy customer has a direct relation to your profits. Here's how important one restaurant feels it is to react positively to a complaining customer.

When a customer is unhappy about some element of his experience at Brennan's restaurants, the manager shows up on their doorstep with a sincere apology and a gift to let the customer know they really value their business. Do you go that far with your customers when they are unhappy about some aspect of your business? You should.

Complaints Are a Wonderful Form of Customer Feedback.

We have discussed other forms of feedback in the previous chapter and how hard it is to obtain. People are so pressured they don't want to take time away from more important tasks to give you feedback. But people **will** take the time to complain. That anger can work to your advantage—if you turn it into a positive.

Here's a classic example that virtually everyone has experienced or witnessed:

The customer entered the jewelry store with a watch that needed repairing. As she was waiting, another customer was complaining to the manager about an underwater watch that wasn't waterproof. It had already been repaired once by the jeweler.

"It still leaks and I want my money back," said the customer rather angrily. "Well, we don't take returns after 30 days and we think it was your fault that it leaked," countered the owner. "But part of that time it was in for repair, and that was definitely not my fault," asserted the customer. The exchange quickly escalated to the shouting stage and the customer finally stormed out shouting that he would never do business with them again.

The other customers in the store looked at each other and several of them, including the customer with a watch to be repaired, left. Would you want to do business with that jewelry store judging by the exchange you just witnessed? Probably not.

Here's another classic:

A grocery chain has instituted self-check out scanners aimed at express customers but, like all technology, it can be temperamental and it takes a few tries to learn how to use it. The store has a cashier conveniently placed in the center of the self-serve aisles who helps out when something is going wrong. Needless to say this person is frequently bombarded from all sides with questions and requests for help. After all, the point of the self-service machines is to get you out of the store quickly.

On a busy pre-Thanksgiving day, a couple checked out about half their order when the scanner stopped scanning. After several polite attempts to get the cashier's attention, they finally succeeded. Instead of getting help, to their surprise, the cashier simply dismissed their problem telling them to "put down" the item that would not scan. Further, she then told them, "I don't care where you put it—just put it down."

The couple was so shocked and enraged they left all the food where it was and walked out. When they encountered the manager, who was busy bagging, and complained, he offered to check them out himself but it was too late.

Because the store is the only large, mid-priced supermarket close to home, the couple had to use it, but if they had an option, they would go elsewhere. In fact, they will drive 20 minutes farther to another market on the other side of town when they can.

What are the lessons here?

First, the best way to handle customer complaints is to avoid them to begin with. A cashier who handles pressure and chaos well might have avoided the incident.

Both of the above stories show that, if the companies took a proactive view of customer complaints, they would still have these customers. They learned the hard (and costly) way that dealing positively with unhappy, complaining customers is often the difference between a company that stays in business and one that does not. Both of the companies are still in business, but not nearly as profitable as they could be.

People must realize that "everywhere you trip is where the treasure lies." Complaints can be a goldmine of information about systems failures or employees who don't do their jobs properly. Successful companies that employ customer service as their competitive-edge use every customer complaint as an opportunity to get better and to learn what customers really want.

Primary reasons customers get upset:

- The customer didn't get what was promised or what was expected

- Someone was rude to the customer

- Someone was indifferent to the customer

- No one listened to and empathized with the customer's problem

- The customer was ignored

- Lack of communication with the customer

- Too much communication with the customer

Are you surprised that complaining can mean that the customer cares about your business? Many times when people complain it means that they want to keep doing business with you, but want you to fix something so they can continue to patronize your business.

When a customer complains about poor service or rude behavior at a restaurant, he is often telling you that he wants to return, and that he wants you to fix that problem so he can come back and dine with you again.

A couple decided to celebrate their anniversary at an elegant, expensive restaurant. Everything was going fine until they were served dessert, a specially ordered soufflé. After the first bite, they looked at each other and quietly put their spoons down. "Do you think this is any good?" queried the wife. "No," said the husband and called for the check. "It's a shame because I would have liked to come back again," he said. It wasn't a very positive ending to what should have been a wonderful occasion.

The waiter approached the table and asked how everything was. At first the couple said everything was "fine." But then the husband decided to complain about the soufflé. He wanted the waiter to know he had always enjoyed the restaurant and would like to come back again.

"Oh, I am so sorry," replied the waiter. "We want to know about things like that." Then he took the soufflé off the bill and offered them something else. He also gave them a gift card good toward a future visit. The couple came back to enjoy many more visits.

This complaint situation is one where the restaurant benefited. They would never have known their previously wonderful soufflés were not measuring up. How many other customers would take the time to complain? Most just never come back.

Complaints will also show you where your employees are falling short in giving superior service to your customers.

A physician's office actively sought feedback in the form of comment cards and phone calls to patients. The analysis of the complaints showed there was one nurse who received many complaints. In fact, one of the patients described her as "Nurse Nasty." Obviously that kind of behavior would not keep patients loyal. So the nurse was coached in how to deliver better service to the practice's patients.

How many other patients would she have driven away if they hadn't asked for patients' complaints? A lot. Most customers do not like to complain and will quietly take their business elsewhere. And the business is left with no idea about why the bottom line is no longer as healthy as it once was.

Complaints show you where systems, equipment and procedures break down.

A customer may experience difficulty navigating your Web site or telephone system. Or the problem may lie in the ordering process or the way a customer moves through the service experience.

A patron visiting a restaurant complained that all the silverware and dishes were dirty. The owner apologized and thanked her for telling him. He came back later to tell the customer that their dishwasher had just broken down, and they had not yet realized it. Was that valuable information for the restaurant? You bet!

Complaints help you learn about "expectation gaps" in your service delivery.

Monica Millican, Division Vice President of CTX Mortgage Compagy, received a complaint from a realtor saying that her home buyer customers were complaining that the broker never returned their calls. It turned out that the mortgage broker's assistant was returning the calls; however the customers' perceptions were that the calls were not being returned by the broker. They expected to receive a call from the mortgage broker herself.

Customer Service: How to Do It Right!

So the assistant is now trained to say, "Monica has asked me to return your call to see if I could help you. We didn't want you to have to wait while Monica was in a meeting." Then, at the end of the call, she asks, "Have I answered all your questions or would you still like for Monica to call you?" This simple change in handling calls, triggered by a customer complaint, helped solve the problem. But they never would have known there was a problem unless they listened to an unhappy customer.

Customers' ideas are often disguised as complaints.

Customers will give you great ideas for future products and services that will help you move ahead of the competition.

- FedEx often heard customers complain that they didn't want to pay the premium price for overnight delivery when all they needed was two-day service. FedEx listened to these complaints and introduced a new form of service called "economy overnight," which is now a major source of revenue for the company.

- A credit union received many complaints from their members that the credit union didn't offer a debit card. So they moved from a plain ATM card to the Master Money Card, which did have a debit function. It made the members happy and increased the credit union's income at the same time. When the credit union instituted Internet interactive banking, members complained that it didn't have a bill-pay function. So they added it and again made their members happy.

- A realtor heard prospective home buyers complain that when they were moving into their new home, there was no place to keep their animals. So the realtor negotiated for a local veterinarian to board the animals at a nominal fee. It was a win-win for everyone involved. The homeowners had a place to economically board their pets and usually became new customers of the vet, while the realtor gained a reputation for exceptional service and many new cheerleaders for her services.

Customers talk about bad experiences more than the good.

Research by TARP indicates that, on average, twice as many people are told about a bad service experience than they are about a good experience. For example, a study conducted for a domestic auto manufacturer revealed that a median of 8 persons were told about a positive outcome of a complaint experience while a median of 16 were told about a bad experience. Customers do talk and they can really hurt business!

How you handle a complaint definitely affects your bottom line. More research by TARP maintains that the ratio of cost to win a new customer versus retaining a current customer varies from 2:1 to 20:1. Furthermore, customers who complain and are satisfied are up to 8 percent more loyal than if they had no problem at all.

Successful handling of complaints creates loyal customers.

A complaining customer whose complaint is satisfactorily resolved will become even more loyal. They will repurchase and refer more business. This is because, until a customer has a problem, the word "service" is just an advertising slogan—something to be distrusted. TARP research shows that up to 70 percent of complainers will return to your business if the complaint is resolved. Up to 95 percent will return if the problem is resolved quickly. When the customer encounters a problem and the company solves it to the customer's satisfaction, that customer thinks, "Wow! They really do have great service." They believe that you walk your talk.

Make it easy for your customers to complain.

Are you eager to hear your customers' complaints, and do you make it easy for them? Or are you like the store manager who, when confronted with a complaining customer, crosses her arms, frowns and says, "How may I help you," with a negative tone of voice. In that simple exchange, the customer feels the manager is not receptive to his complaint and makes him so uncomfortable that he never returns to the store again.

John Burg, President and Owner of John Burg Air Depot, an air conditioning firm, asks his technicians to leave a Better Business Bureau survey at every job. When they are forwarded to the company, the technician is rewarded with $1.00 for every one that comes in.

"If a survey indicates that the customer was not happy, for example, if the service person was not on time, we call and speak with the customer and usually offer him a discount certificate. This gives us a chance to show the customer that we can do it right, and this hopefully keeps the customer coming back to us instead of going to a competitor," Burg says.

As mentioned in Chapter Three, be sure you make it easy for customers to complain. Are comment cards easily accessible? If you have offices in multiple states or locations within the state, do you have an 800 number for your customers to call when they have a problem? Do you regularly use some of the customer feedback methods discussed in the previous chapter?

If you make it difficult for the customer to complain, not only will they be angrier when they finally reach you, you will miss some complaints from those who are not as persistent.

Respond quickly to all customer complaints.

Jim Saxe, owner of Putt-Putt Fun House in Houston, Texas, says, "The worst thing to do is not to jump on the problem and see what you can do immediately." He empowers everyone on his staff to deal with a complaint when it occurs. They don't have to go looking for their shift leader or manager in order to appease the customer. Empowering your employees is an important part of dealing quickly with all complaints.

Saxe sets parameters, of course. Employees cannot do anything against safety or insurance rules, like letting a child ride the bumper boats if he is not tall enough. However, they can use tokens for any of the amusements to calm customers who are unhappy with some aspect of their experience.

Saxe believes that if his employees' methods make sense and are rational, they should be empowered to do it. And quickly. "Otherwise, the customer will make a scene and escalate the problem, so that it takes two or three people's time to solve it instead of just one person," says Saxe.

It's also important to deal quickly with written complaints. Have you ever written a letter of complaint, only to receive no reply or a form letter? It probably made you mad. And it may have taken a long time to receive any reply at all.

Respond quickly to all angry customers, and personalize your response as much as possible. Don't send a form letter that does not mention the customer's specific concerns. It will be perceived as a "push my button" letter. That kind of letter often does not even have the name personalized. It starts with "Dear Sir or Madam" and makes the customer even angrier and more difficult to deal with. The customer ends up feeling they are just a number and the company does not really care about their complaint.

Here is an example of what <u>not</u> to do.

Dear Sir or Madam;

I am writing in response to your concern regarding XYZ Company. I am sorry to hear of your less than satisfactory experience with us. We apologize for the inconvenience. I have copied your letter and distributed it to the manager of the appropriate department so your observations and insights can be addressed.

If you received this letter, would you be mollified? Would you think that XYZ Company really cared about your complaint? Of course not!

The letter should be personalized with the complaining customer's name and the specific incident the customer is complaining about. The name and department the letter was copied to should also be stated. It should say that the manager will be calling the person within a certain amount of time to address the complaint. Then make sure it happens!

Marshall Field, the founder of the famous store based in Chicago said, "Those who buy support me, those who come to flatter me, please me. Those who complain teach me how I may please others so that they will buy. Only those hurt me who are displeased but do not complain. They refuse me permission to correct my errors and thus improve my service."

So use the complaints you receive from your customers to improve poor service in your business. Look for patterns in the comments and draw up a list of your most common complaints. Then address and fix them. Because if a customer complains about something and you don't fix it, they will definitely not come back, and they will tell many of their friends not to either.

RATE YOURSELF:

Rate your company on its complaint handling. Note areas where you need to improve.

Check the appropriate box:	Yes	No
My company has an easily-understood policy regarding customer complaints.	❏	❏
All my employees have been trained in how to handle customer complaints.	❏	❏
All customers are treated the same—we do not make an exception for one while not for the other.	❏	❏
We document all complaints.	❏	❏
We bring all complaints to the attention of the department responsible.	❏	❏
All complaints are analyzed by management to see how the root cause of the problem can be eliminated.	❏	❏
Employees are kept informed about how complaints are resolved.	❏	❏
Our company regularly surveys lost customers as to why they left.	❏	❏
Someone from management follows up on each complaint to make sure it was satisfactorily resolved.	❏	❏

Scoring:

9-8 yeses = You are doing well. Keep it up.

7-5: yeses = Your complaint handling and procedures need to be improved.

Less than 5 yeses = You are probably losing customers because of poor complaint handling. Try to implement some of the above actions soon.

CHAPTER SIX

Learning Complaint-Handling Skills

Clearly, one key element of effective customer service is learning how to "handle" complaints without losing a customer.

Effective "complaint defense" is often the hardest part of your job. Today customers are more empowered by consumer advocates, media exposure and government regulations. If it seems that customers are doing more complaining today—they are.

Add to this the fact that no one is perfect. No business gets it right 100 percent of the time. There are times when things will go wrong. (You can also depend on it being during the height of a rush too.)

What happens is up to you. Planning for disaster is the best "defense." Think worst case scenario always: the sight of a disgruntled customer walking away and vowing to tell everyone about their negative experience.

You can, however, change this scenario. You can handle her so skillfully that she walks away feeling that you simply made a mistake that won't reoccur. It's usually a matter of what you say and how you say it rather than what you "give" the customer.

The ability to deal with rude, unhappy customers is a key skill for both managers and employees. There are really only two ways to handle complaints:

- The hard way

- The easy way

The hard way is to push back on the customer with the "caveman" response, and escalate the complaint into a full-fledged confrontation.

The easy way is to follow certain steps that will diffuse the situation, calm the customer and resolve the situation to the customer's satisfaction so that he will continue to be your customer.

Below are the steps that you must follow in order to deal successfully with an unhappy customer and establish an effective "complaint defense" program.

Step One: Prepare Yourself Mentally.

Keep in mind that it usually isn't about you. This will help you avoid taking the complaint personally. Generally, customers have "expectations" that are not met, whether it's product failure, poor technical assistance, or simply feeling they've been taken advantage of.

People who are able to handle complaining customers in a positive way step outside of themselves and act as an observer of their own actions. This is easier than you think. A good exercise is to remember a particular incident that worked well when you handled a complaining customer.

- What did you do or say that made the encounter go well?

- What were you thinking as you dealt with the complaint?

- What kind of stress had you been subjected to that day—a lot or very little?

- Were you in a good mood or a bad mood?

Take apart that previous encounter action-by-action, word-by-word to see why it was a successful encounter with an unhappy customer.

Now think of a time when the opposite was true.

- What did you do and say differently?

- What made the difference between a situation that went well versus one that went not-so-well?

Next, check your body language.

- Is it closed, with arms crossed?

- Are you frowning?

- Do you have a negative expression on your face?

If you are dealing with your angry customer in person, poor body language will get things off on the wrong foot. It will also carry through in your tone of voice if you are dealing with the customer on the telephone. **Make sure your body language is open with arms uncrossed and palms up. Keep your facial expression neutral**.

Commit to what is called the "adult" behavior state. This is where you think, "I am here to help this customer. We have a problem and I am here to solve it." Avoid the scolding teacher approach where you tell the customer things like, "Well, you should have read the guarantee," or "If you had just let us know sooner, we could have done something about the problem."

Remember, "He who angers you conquers you." Anger is a choice that you make. No one can <u>make</u> you angry; you allow yourself to become angry. Avoid the "caveman response"—pushing back on the customer—because you feel threatened.

- Remember that angry customers are unhappy with your organization, not you. But, at this moment, you represent the organization.

- Dealing successfully with unhappy people is a mind game. It starts in your head and you *decide* how to respond to that angry customer.

- Imagine there is a glass wall between you and the angry customer. When the customer says something critical or hurtful, picture it bouncing off your protective wall. Nothing can hurt you.

TIPS ON ANGER CONTROL:

1. **Identify what triggered your anger.** Did the customer call you "stupid" or make you feel stupid? Did they raise their voice? What did they say that "gotcha?" Compose a list of things that make you angry and push your "hot button." Recognizing your hot buttons will help you avoid reacting to them in the future.

2. **Remind yourself that you, not the angry customer, are in control.** Resist the urge to respond immediately. Take a deep breath and wait a few seconds before you respond. Repeat something the customer has said to give you time to calm down.

Customer Service: How to Do It Right!

3. **Ask for someone else's opinion if possible.** See what their reaction would be. Get some perspective on the situation.

4. **Take a quick "time out" if possible.** Get a cup of coffee, use the restroom or work on another task for a few minutes. Anything to divert your focus from the angry customer will help you cool down and solve the situation—not make it worse.

Step Two: "Let 'Em Blow!"

This means let them state what is bothering them. Don't interrupt and make excuses or give reasons at this point of the encounter. Just let them vent. An upset customer is a lot like a pressure cooker—if you don't let them vent, they will explode. You must always deal with the person and their feelings first, and then the problem, if you are to successfully deal with an angry customer.

Here's a personal anecdote:

I picked up the telephone and before I could even say, "Hello", the person on the other end of the line was heatedly saying,

"You have the stupidest organization I have ever seen!" The caller on the other end of the phone was complaining about a volunteer organization of which I was president. It seems that he had called the membership director three times to get information about joining the organization but had not yet received anything.

I quickly moved into problem-solving mode and promised to get him something overnight. That's where I made a mistake. I didn't let him vent first; I moved too quickly to fix the problem and skipped an important step in dealing with angry customers. He needed to let off some steam first.

So instead of calming down when I promised what he wanted, he just became angrier. Realizing my mistake, I asked more questions and listened patiently to his complaint. Only after I had done that was he able to talk reasonably about his problem.

And, needless to say, I made sure he got his membership information the next day. I also followed up with a call that turned him from a negative to a positive, resulting in a new member.

This is a classic example of how important it is to fix the person first. You must let them vent their anger and then, only then, deal with the problem. This is a critical skill in handling unhappy people. Oddly enough, many people do just the opposite. They jump to solve the problem right away. If you do so, you're missing one of the most important steps in dealing with unhappy people.

Think of it as letting them ascend a volcano of anger. After all, when customers are mad, they are somewhat like a volcano. They climb up the volcano, rumbling and complaining, making sarcastic comments and sometimes behaving in a rude manner. This usually makes it difficult for you to keep your cool. Eventually they get to the top, blow and then start their descent toward calmness. Relax. This is just part of the procedure. It is a way to let the person blow off steam. Don't skip this step, or you will not be able to deal effectively with your angry customer.

While the customer is shouting, making rude remarks and generally being hard to deal with, listen actively. This means making the customer feel you are really listening to him by using good eye contact, giving him your undivided attention and exhibiting other open body language cues such as uncrossing your arms. This makes the customer feel you care about his problem and you want to do something about it.

Give verbal feedback like "I see..." "Go on," "And then what happened?" Use meaningless words, grunts and phrases like "Uh-huh," "Mmm" and so on. This is especially important when you are dealing with a complaint on the telephone, because you can't use your body language as part of your message.

Have you ever spoken to someone on the phone and heard them say, "Are you still there?" That is usually a clue that you haven't been giving the person enough verbal feedback. Be sure to let the customer know you are listening and care about the problem by giving verbal feedback.

As they calm down, ask, "Is there anything else?"

You **always** want to ask for more, so you can be sure to get all the details of the cause of the anger. Keep asking, "Is that all?" until they sputter out. Often the only thing a customer really wants is a chance to be heard and to be told that you are as upset as they are about the problem.

Step Three: Try to Develop Rapport with the Customer.

This makes them easier to deal with. Keep the mental attitude that you are there to fix the problem strongly in your mind.

This is also the right time to apologize for their inconvenience and explain why the problem occurred. **If you do this before they vent, however, they will not listen to you, and your excuses will make them even angrier**.

If the problem occurred because another department goofed up, don't blame it on them—after all, blame shifting is not your job, and it won't make the customer any happier. Simply apologize. When you blame another department, it makes the customer uneasy, and he will question the capability of the entire organization, not just the shipping department. Use sincere statements that will develop some rapport with the customer like:

- Oh, I am **so** sorry about your inconvenience.

- I would be angry if that happened to me, too.

- I'm sorry this happened, but I'm glad you're bringing this to our attention.

- I can understand how upset this situation has made you.

This will help get the customer on your side and become more reasonable and open to problem solving. And when you agree with the customer about their frustrations, they will have a hard time staying mad at you. After all, it's hard to continue to argue with someone who is agreeing with you!

Use the person's name. "I'm very sorry about this, Mrs. Smith." Even though it is not your fault, it is important to apologize as a representative of your organization.

Ask questions and repeat back some things the customer said. This will assure the customer that you were listening to him and you truly understand his problem. For example:

- Let me make sure I understand the problem. You are unhappy with the turn-around time.

- Am I correct in understanding that you did not like your meal?

Sometimes the previous steps take seconds or several minutes. Don't skip those first three steps even if you are busy and needed elsewhere, or you will never be able to truly satisfy your customer.

Remember: it's crucial to deal with the angry customer's *feelings* first, then solve the problem. If you simply address the facts and don't address the customer's anger about their inconvenience, embarrassment or loss of time, you will still have an angry customer.

Steps 1-3 help **fix the person.** Only after you deal with the customer's feelings can you move toward **fixing the problem.**

Step Four: Create the Solution—Fix the Problem.

Once your customer has vented and you are sure you understand the problem, move into problem solving.

Try saying something like, "Let's see what we can do to solve your problem." If possible, let the customer suggest what he wants you to do. Ask, "What would you like to see us do in this situation?" This can quickly calm the customer and will help you get an idea of what the customer is expecting you to do.

If you can't do what the customer wants, offer alternatives. Customers like to have choices, and it gives them a sense of control about the situation. But be sure to discuss the alternatives fully so you are sure they understand. Irate, upset customers often do not listen well.

A customer needed to return a gift to a local department store, but since she didn't have a receipt she anticipated a problem. Walking up to the desk, she told the clerk, "I would like to return this dress." Sure enough, the first thing the clerk asked was, "Do you have your receipt?"

Defensively, the customer answered, "No, it was a gift." "Well," replied the clerk with a bright smile, "You have two choices then; you can either select something else or receive a voucher good for future merchandise. Which would you rather do?"

The customer took a deep breath and smiled back. A difficult situation was easily solved by the technique of making the customer feel she had choices.

Always tell the customer exactly what you are going to do in terms of specific actions, not just outcomes. Don't say, "I'll take care of it." Instead, tell the customer exactly what you will do to solve their problem. "I will call the shipping department and let you know something by 3:00 p.m."

Don't think that you have to "give away the store" to make your customer happy. Often a customer will be satisfied by much less than you think. But don't ever let a customer walk away without first trying to satisfy them in some way.

What does this mean? It can be some small token. For example, a dentist has small gifts of fragrances and soap for his female patients. Restaurants can offer a free drink or dessert or a coupon good for a future visit. (This is particularly good since their future visit will likely be a much better experience. Recall the story of the pizza place from Chapter 4.)

Finally, check back with your customer to make sure they were satisfied with the complaint resolution. This is a very important step that will impress your customer and hopefully completely smooth over the poor service incident.

Watch out, however, for raising the customer's expectations. If you do it once, you may have to do it again or for other customers. You have just raised the bar. If you make a special effort to rush things through on an order, the customer may expect that again. Sometimes you have to say "no" to a customer.

How to say "no" to a customer—the right way.

1. Listen to all they have to say about the problem. Don't interrupt.

2. Apologize and say "I'm so sorry, if we could do that for you we would. Unfortunately, we can't and here is the reason why." (Explain the reasons.)

   • "I'm sorry, I wish we could do that, but unfortunately, government regulations do not allow us to release medical records to anyone but the patient."

   • "I apologize. In order to be fair to all our customers, we need to take the requests in the order received."

3. Offer alternatives, if possible.

- "If you will bring your wife in, I can then release the records to her."

- "Let's see if we have any other options."

4. Apologize once again that you could not do what the customer wanted.

Other don'ts

- Don't complain to customers about the previous difficult customer. They will wonder if they will be the next one talked about.

- Avoid "fire starter" phrases that just escalate the complaint into a major fire.

Instead of:

- "You have to…"

- "You'll have to talk to customer service about that."

- "It's against our policy."

- "It's not my job."

- "You should have…"

Say:

- "Let me tell you who can help you with that. Please go down the hall to customer service."

- "I'm so sorry, if we could do that for you we would. Let me tell you what we can do."

- "I'm sorry, that is not in my area. Let me tell you (or connect you to) the person who can help you with that."

Or…

- "Let me see what I can do to help."

- "Let me see what I can do for you right now. The next time, it would make it easier on you if you brought all your paperwork."

There are generally two kinds of complaints—those that can be made right and those that can't. And often they are both. For instance, if you delivered the wrong couch to a customer, you can go back, get the right one and redeliver it. That can be fixed.

But what you can't make right is the time the customer had to spend waiting for the delivery. You can never give them back that extra time, so you need to compensate for it in some way. A profuse, sincere apology is a good start. If you can give them a coupon good for a percentage off of a future purchase, that is even better. It says to the customer, "We are really sorry about the mix-up."

When you deal effectively with angry customers, you will accomplish a positive "service recovery." That's when you keep your customer loyal by satisfying their complaint. It means transforming a dissatisfied customer into a satisfied one even though you messed up. When you use these steps in dealing with complaining customers, you will avoid escalating the complaint to a full-fledged fire.

But sometimes you can use all of the above techniques and the customer is still very abusive and demands unreasonable things. They are often called "terrorist customers." The first step is to call on your manager to step in. Often, the customer will become more agreeable when speaking to a higher level manager. And just the little time it takes for the manager to arrive often calms down the customer and makes him easier to deal with.

Hopefully, the manager will back up what you have already said, or the customer will quickly learn that the higher up he goes, the more he will get. Word will quickly get around, and customers will soon be bypassing your customer service representative and trying to go as high up as they can in order to get more.

RATE YOURSELF ON HOW WELL YOU HANDLE COMPLAINTS:

	Always	Sometimes	Never

1. I listen carefully to the customer's complaint before I try to solve it.

2. I am able to take complaints professionally, not personally.

3. I value complaints as an opportunity to win back the customer and to see where things are going wrong.

4. I keep an open body language when dealing with irate customers.

5. I am able to apologize to the unhappy customer even if the problem is not my fault.

6. I am able to say "no" to a customer in a tactful way.

Scoring:

6 yeses = You are a pro at handling complaints.

5-4 yeses = You have good skills, but need some improvement.

Less than 4 yeses = Your complaint-handling skills need to be improved. Pick two of the skills above and work on them with your next complaining customer. Keep doing that until you have mastered all the skills.

The Basic Rules About Customer Complaints

- Respond quickly to all customer communications

- Believe that solving a customer's problem is an important investment in your business

- Give all your people who deal with external customers training in complaint handling and service recovery

- Follow the steps of the "complaint defense"

- Avoid "push a button" responses—form letters or phrases that make the customer feel like a number

- Make sure that complaining customers are always respected and treated accordingly, even if they are wrong

CHAPTER SEVEN

Hiring for Customer Service Success

"Customer service superiority begins with whom we hire, how we hire them and how we bring them into our organization. Customer service positions cannot be made 'idiot-proof' to be delivered by robots. You must have thinking, caring individuals in service positions. So you must hire the right people in the first place."

Robert Desatnik, noted customer service expert

Unemployed for three months, Paul spotted a sign on the door of a small marine repair business, and after asking politely, is shown into the owner's office. The job, the owner explains is more than a parts person; it involves a lot of customer service and requires a person with patience and good humor. They often have customers who don't know exactly what they are looking for and are in a hurry and a bad mood. It also happens that the company has had this opening for a while, having lost a long-term employee to retirement.

Because they really needed to fill the position (Paul was well spoken, had a good education and was well groomed) the owner asked only a few more questions. Paul was hired immediately and started work the next day.

The first incident came quickly when a customer who spoke a combination of English and Spanish seemed to be having trouble finding a product. After several attempts to point him in the right direction, the customer cursed Paul (in Spanish) and left the store. While the owner was concerned, he decided to give Paul the chance to get into the job and not criticize him.

Paul had no further problems until a few days later when the owner overheard a conversation he was having with a customer on the phone. While he couldn't hear both sides, it was clear that Paul wasn't paying attention, essentially blowing off the customer and finally hanging up with a "take it or leave it" answer.

At this point, the owner decided to keep a close watch on Paul, and it quickly became apparent that even though Paul seemed nice in the interview, he was not nice to customers. He had a chip on his shoulder and looked down on people who did not know exactly what they needed. Paul simply was not cut out for customer service and was let go the next week.

Could the problem—not to mention the lost goodwill—have been prevented with a better interviewing and hiring process? Obviously, but this is a procedure that requires careful thought and planning. It's not enough to find good employees—but good employees with the patience and personality for customer service. With careful interviewing, you will avoid many of the mistakes that are made in hiring, and end up with employees who deliver excellent service for your company and stay with you longer.

Some thoughts about using your hiring process to become a service leader:

1. You need to take as much care in hiring customer service employees as you would in selecting a high-level manager.

2. You must look for people whose personalities predispose them to produce good service and to fit in well with the culture of your organization.

3. More simply put: hire people who just naturally want to give good service.

4. Recognize and admit that not everyone is equipped to deal with the public in a customer service capacity. Not everyone can be trained to deliver customer service, no matter how much time and money you spend. Some people just are not suited for it.

5. Some people are just naturally better at it than others. Dealing with customers in a positive manner is a basic talent. And those are the employees you want to find and hire.

Follow this process to help you achieve these steps.

Establishing a Hiring Process:
Do it right the first time.

In order to consistently deliver superior customer service, you must develop a hiring process that will result in employing people who will be successful in dealing with your customers—even if that person will have other duties. Despite your busy schedule, it is critical to make the time to conduct a good interview because it deserves as much or more attention as you give to the rest of your business. In your rush to find people for your service positions, you must resist the urge to hire the first warm body that walks in the door and is reasonably qualified. After all, if you don't have the time to do it right the first time, when will you have the time to do it over? Not to mention all the lost customers that will result from a bad hire.

Sure, you can train anyone in the basic skills of customer service, and a future chapter will discuss this. But if the prospective employee doesn't have a natural people orientation to start with, he will never be the kind of service provider who can deliver the kind of service that will attract new customers, help you keep the ones you have and be the differentiator that makes your company stand out from all the others.

Here are some things to include in your hiring process so that you will consistently hire people that can be trained to excel in customer service.

1. Develop Job Specifications:

Before you conduct your first interview, the most important thing is to determine the job requirements and describe, in detail, the person you want to fill the job.

Begin by asking yourself a simple question. As a customer, what skills and behaviors do I expect in a person providing exceptional customer service in this business? While you may have a clear picture in mind—it may not be the person who will best serve your customer base.

Mel Kleiman, President of Humetrics, a firm specializing in hiring, and author of "Hire Tough," says that choosing the right employee for a specific spot is much like an experience in a grocery store. "What is the most important thing to take to the grocery store other than money and coupons?" he asks. "A list. What happens when you forget the list," he questions? "You don't get everything you need, you get things you really don't need, you spend more money than you planned, you spend more time than you've planned and you forget something you need and have to go back and do it again."

And that's exactly what happens when you interview candidates without a list of what you need and want according to Kleiman. You forget to ask the questions you need answered and you ask some that are irrelevant. So before you go shopping for your next employee, make a list. Identify what's important and then interview for those skills.

Start with a simple shopping list of the basics needed:

SKILLS: What amount of knowledge and skills are required to perform each duty? Must they be already in place or can they be taught? If you don't have much time to get new hires up to speed, for example before Christmas in a retail store, you obviously need to search for candidates who already posses the needed skills. Or if they must use customer service software, do you have time to teach them? **How skillful do they need to be in each area?** Is "some knowledge" okay? Or do they need to be at least an intermediate level or even advanced?

CAPACITY: What are the major responsibilities of the job and the critical duties of each? These can be make or break factors, such as they must be able to work nights or weekends, lift up to 30 pounds and other basics. Can they read and carry out simple written instructions? What else is critical to the job? Without these abilities, they won't be able to do the job well.

ATTITUDES: This is the hardest thing to discover. Does the person have a naturally positive attitude that will transfer into outstanding customer service skills? Do they feel that serving other people is important and not beneath them? You should use behavior-based interviewing, discussed later in this chapter, to uncover the candidate's basic attitudes. And remember Paul, who seemed to be a good potential CS employee, but once he was put in the "arena," his defensive and somewhat hostile attitude emerged.

Here are some other questions to ask yourself as you put together the job specifications:

- What hiring mistakes have you made in the past?

- Do you need a different type of person because the job has changed (i.e., more computer skills or skills required to take orders or cross-sell other products and services)?

- Is it important that your new hire have a warm, friendly phone voice? If so, then the first interview should be by telephone.

- Do they need to be quick in completing a transaction, as in the express lane of a grocery store? If so, you should observe the individual carefully during the interview to see how quickly he or she moves and speaks.

- Do they need good listening skills, an ability to get to the core of a problem and then take the initiative to solve it?

- Do you need a person who is very accurate because the job involves a lot of critical numbers as in the payroll department? Making a mistake on an internal customer's paycheck is definitely not good customer service.

The time you spend deciding on the exact job specifications will result in employees who stay with you longer, fit the job better and thus give better performance to help keep your customers.

2. Go Beyond Simple Surface Assessments: Look Below the Surface.

Look carefully at your best employees. What, exactly, makes them successful? Are they always smiling and using good eye contact? In that case, look for job candidates who do the same in the interview. Is there something about their facial expression that is particularly welcoming? Notice their face "in park." That's when their natural resting position takes over. Would it portray a positive or negative impression to your customers? Try to isolate the qualities that make your current employees successful, and then look for those same qualities in your job prospects.

Consider using personality assessment tests.

If you have the budget, there are many consultant services available that will develop a computerized aptitude survey. Through research, they determine what qualities make up a desirable customer contact person in that particular position and then draw up a profile to fit your organization. This will zero in on exactly what you want to look for in a customer service representative.

Next, they select standardized tests that measure the behaviors they have identified as your success factors. They validate these tests by giving them to your existing, successful employees. Finally, the consultant will select those items on which your people scored well and combine them into a test for you.

Your industry association may have some industry-wide specifications for you to use. Consider getting your employees, the ones who are actually performing the services, to help you with this. They can often zero in on the behaviors and skills much faster than you, and they may pick up on some skills you have missed.

Use more than the one-person interview.

Many companies have their employees do part of the interviewing and give them input into the final selection. This way, the employees feel they have a stake in making the new employee successful. After all, they helped select her!

One company has a rigorous three-part interview process. First, the Human Relations manager interviews the applicant with one other employee in the room. Next, two other employees plus the HR manager take part in the interview. Finally, a third interview involves yet another employee as well as the director. By the time the potential hire gets to the third interview, he has relaxed enough for his real personality to show. You can bet any candidate who can make it through this process will probably be outstanding!

Another company ends the interview with the potential employee having refreshments and doing some socializing with other employees. Unbeknownst to the candidate, those employees are also evaluating him. They often get information that the interviewer didn't, because the applicant was on her "best behavior" in the actual interview.

Still other companies have the receptionist start to evaluate the candidate the minute she walks in the door. How did she treat the receptionist? Was she nice or did she treat her badly?

The Bottom Line: All the service skills you need are based on two key items: what customers expect, and your company's service strategy. You can also use your service targets or goals to match up the candidate with the job specifications. This is why establishing a service vision is so important.

3. The Interviewing Process: You Must Have a Game Plan Before You Begin.

Some suggestions/options:

- Prepare (well ahead of the interview) an individualized interview plan for each applicant to ensure that you get the information you need.

- Study the applicant's general qualifications and work history from the employment application or résumé.

- Decide what additional information or clarification you need.

- Formulate questions that will help you fill the gap.

- List the other questions you will want to ask.

- Review what information about the job and the company you will need to provide to the candidate.

- Be honest and don't sugarcoat the job—tell both the pluses and minuses. For example, if they will be asked to take abuse from many angry customers, you need to bring this up. Probe to see how they feel about it. This will help weed out the less-qualified candidates ahead of time.

One well-known hotel reservations department has discovered an upside to describing many of the negatives of the job; reduced turnover. For example, potential new hires are told that customers hang up on them and verbally abuse them when the room they want is not available. The employees are thus well prepared for what they may encounter. Of course, management also sells the positive job benefits, so it doesn't appear to be all negative.

When you are honest about the "real life" customer situations employees can expect to encounter, you end up hiring people who are better matched to the position and who are likely to be more successful and stay longer.

4. Test Your Candidates' Skills.

Give job applicants an assignment to do before they come to the interview. Have them write a brief letter answering these three points:

1. Why they want the job.

2. What strengths they will bring to the job.

3. Define what exceptional customer service means to them.

If they make the effort to do that, you will know that they already have some of the characteristics necessary to perform well, like follow-through. This also indicates a good attitude.

If they are already trained in a specific skill, ask them to perform the actual job while you observe. (Remember, though, you must then have every candidate perform that same test in order to avoid legal problems.)

5. Remember That You Will Be Judged Too

Don't forget to sell the positive aspects of working for your company. Treat the applicant well. He could be a future customer. So be sure to start the interview on time, treat all applicants the same, work to establish rapport just as you would with a customer and show respect for the candidate, even if you know from the beginning that he is not right for the job.

Chuck Robinson, a manager at a Putt-Putt FunHouse, includes a message in information given to people "trying out" for a spot on his party team. It sets a positive tone for the interview. (He also does group interviews to see how the people interact with others.)

"Welcome to Putt-Putt FunHouse. My name is Chuck Robinson, and today we have invited you to experience our kind of fun and to find out if this working environment is what you are looking for. This "tryout interview" is designed to introduce you to the Putt-Putt FunHouse birthday party concept. Be prepared to learn about us, and feel free to ask as many questions as you can. It is from this "Tryout interview" that we will select our new party team members. We will be playing games, talking about different scenarios that might come up and we will also be sampling some of the FunHouse Café's excellent food! Thanks for making the effort to come out today, and I hope you have fun while you are here!"

He also includes a detailed schedule for the interview so that everyone will know what to expect.

6. Ask the Right Questions for Different Kinds Of Interviews.

Use an organized approach and ask the same questions of each candidate, except those relating to the résumé or application blank, so you can compare. Without this approach you cannot equally judge each applicant. Whether the interview is in person or on the telephone, check to see how the answers fit into your job specifications worksheet.

If the job entails working unusual hours (e.g., evenings), schedule the interview for that time of day. One tire dealer does only early morning and late afternoon interviews because their customers come in before and after work, and those are the times when employees must be their sharpest.

Your questioning skills are very important in the interviewing process. Here are a few kinds of questions you can use:

Open-ended questions: A question that needs more than a "yes," "no," or a "few words" answer. This will get the candidate talking at length. Here are some examples:

- What is the greatest challenge you have ever faced?

- Tell me about a time you got bad service, what you did and how you handled it.

- Tell me about a time you got great customer service and what made it so great.

- What does it take to be a great (put in job title)?

- Tell me a little bit about why you left your last job.

- How was your relationship with your supervisor?

- Describe any disagreements you had with your coworkers.

- What attracts you to the job for which you are applying?

- Tell me about the kind of customer contact you have had. Describe a typical day.

- What do you enjoy most about dealing with customers?

- What do you consider most important when working with customers?

- What have you done in the past that reflects your enjoyment of people in general?

- Tell me how you recently used your sense of humor in a difficult situation.

Mel Kleiman, President of Humetrics

"Our first jobs shape our work ethic and habits. How young the person was, why they took the job, how difficult it was, and how long they stuck with it all tell you something about an applicant's character. My favorite interviewing question is 'What was your first paying job and what three things did it teach you?'"

Close-ended questions: These are used to gather information that is factual and objective. Often they can be answered with a simple yes or no or a few facts. They get exactly the information you need, but fail to provide much depth of information, unless the interviewee chooses to elaborate.

Here are some examples:

- When could you begin work if you are hired?

- What were your specific job duties?

- What were your hours?

- How many days of work or school did you miss last year?

- Are you able to work weekends? Nights?

- Will wearing a uniform bother you?

- What training or qualifications do you have for this job?

- What one word would you like people to use in describing your work in customer service?

Not all questions need to be lengthy. Use few words and short questions to get the applicant to give you more information. For example:

- How so?

- What type of customer service training have you had?

- And then what did you do?

- Um hum.

- Yes?

- Why do you feel that way?

- The echoing techniques of repeating back to the candidate what they just said. "So you liked the people contact in your last job?"

- Silence. People tend to fill pauses with words, and your applicant will often add more unplanned information if you remain quiet for a few seconds.

The behavior-based interview: Probing questions are used here in order to select the best candidates for your service-oriented positions. This kind of interviewing is especially important in evaluating the "soft skills" like teamwork, attitude and other customer service capabilities.

If you want an employee to solve customer-related problems without having to consult a supervisor, ask a question like, "Tell me about a time when you had a problem with a customer and how you solved it." Or, "Let me give you a typical customer problem, and tell me how you would solve it."

Putt-Putt FunHouse uses these interview scenarios:

- You are hosting a party when you find out that the pizza is going to be late. What do you do?

- Everything has gone wrong with your party, some of which is not your fault, and the party mom is very upset. How would you handle this?

- There is one party guest who constantly tries to take all the attention away from the birthday child. What do you do to control the situation?

Some other examples are:

- Tell me about a time when you had to get along with a variety of people in order to get things done.

- Describe a situation when you were able to calm an angry customer.

- Tell me about a time when you were unable to satisfy a difficult customer.

- Tell me about a time you went the extra mile for a customer.

- Think of a time you have seen another person show poor judgment with a customer. Describe what happened.

The first-job interview: If you are interviewing someone who has no previous job experience, alter the questions and have them relate the question to their experiences at school, with friends or any school activities or clubs.

For instance, you could ask, "Tell me about the teacher you like best, and why?" "Tell me about a time when you were able to calm someone who was angry." Or relate the questions to their own experiences as customers. "Tell me about a time you received bad customer service. How did you feel? What did you do about it?" Look at how they dealt with the situation. Did they behave in a mature and adult manner, or as a child, taking it personally? That's the way they will act with your customers!

Another important thing to remember is that résumés don't always tell the whole story. And sometimes candidates are less than honest on them. Spend some time talking about what they did on their previous job. Listen carefully for the things that will fit into your job specifications worksheet.

- Tell me about a typical day on your last job.

- What did you like doing the most in your previous job?

- What was the least favorite part of your last job?

Phone screening interviews: When you have a lot of applicants, phone screening can save you time. Plus, if the position will include some phone work, you can get a sense of how customer-friendly their voice is.

Role-playing actual situations they will encounter in their work is helpful either in person or on the telephone. Read from a script of an actual conversation in which a customer is looking for what you sell or has a problem that needs to be resolved. Have the applicant ask you questions as if you were the customer. If the employee will have to deal with irate customers, be sure to role-play that too.

Here Are Some Sample Questions to Use on the Telephone:

Do's:

- What made you respond to the ad?

- What kind of experience do you have?

- What do you think it takes to make a good employee?

- What hours and days would you prefer to work?

- Of all the work or life experience you have, where have you been the most successful?

Don'ts

- Don't talk too much. You will learn more about the candidate if you let them talk. Spend 80 percent of the interview listening.

- Don't waste precious interview time describing the job and the kind of person you are looking for. All that does is reveal to the candidate the answers you want to hear.

- Don't make a hire/don't hire decision within the first 30 seconds of meeting the candidate, as most people do. This is a gut reaction to be avoided at all costs.

- Don't ask illegal questions. Keep up with all the changes in the law that affect hiring.

- Don't seem rushed. Move the interview at a moderate pace and try not to look at your watch.

- Don't forget that applicants will be on their very best behavior. Work your system to unearth the real person and her personality.

Other Tricks of the Trade:

- A major airline brings all job candidates together in a room and has each person make a presentation to the group. But they don't evaluate the speaker. Instead, they watch the audience to see who is attentive and supportive of the speaker. This helps them to see which candidates seem to care about others, a key skill in delivering exceptional customer service.

- A hotel chain excludes all candidates who smile fewer than four times during the interview.

- A fast-food business pays particular attention to the applicant's body language. They look for proper eye contact, leaning forward to show interest and smiling. If they don't exhibit them in the interview, they are excluded.

7. Rate Candidates on the Characteristics You Need.

Often, with competing and equal candidates, you may want to select the characteristics you feel are the most important in order for you to make a decision.

Are sales skills the most important? Give it 40 percent. What about verbal skills? Good phone voice and manner? A friendly person who smiles a lot? Give each a percentage. Continue until all characteristics are weighted in percentages and the total equals 100 percent. Then, on a scale of one through five, with five being the best, rate how each candidate meets these needs. Finally multiply this by the weight to determine the candidate's score for each characteristic.

Even if you have only one qualified candidate, complete this exercise. It will help you determine who will be successful in your environment.

Kleiman recommends using the **C•A•P•S** approach:

Capacity   Does the candidate have the mental and physical capabilities to do the job?

Attitude   Is the candidate willing to perform and produce on the job?

Personality   Will the candidate's personality fit the position and the organization?

Skill   Does the candidate have the skills necessary to perform the job?

HIRE FOR ATTITUDE, TRAIN FOR SKILLS

Don't forget to check the references. Besides the usual phone call, Teresa Sedeno, a consultant with Dynamic Synergy Associates, uses an original approach. She calls the references at a time when she thinks they won't be there and leaves the following message. "I would like you to call me if this person is really outstanding." If the reference calls back, she knows she has a winner!

Think all this takes too much time? Figure out the cost of losing an employee, plus the time spent finding a new one and think again. Choosing the best candidate the first time will result in improved customer service and less cost for you. That's worth an investment of your time, isn't it?

RATE YOURSELF QUIZ

1. Do I study a candidate's résumé and prepare personalized questions based on that résumé?	Always	Sometimes	Never
2. Do I have everyone fill out an application blank before I interview them?	Always	Sometimes	Never
3. Do I avoid jumping to conclusions based on the candidate's appearance?	Always	Sometimes	Never
4. Do I hire according to the job specifications instead of hiring someone "just like me?"	Always	Sometimes	Never
5. Do I use mostly open-ended questions that encourage the candidates to express goals, values and feelings?	Always	Sometimes	Never
6. Do I listen carefully to each candidate's response rather than trying to think of the next question?	Always	Sometimes	Never
7. Do I keep my questions short, so I am not likely to influence the answer?	Always	Sometimes	Never

Scoring:

7-6 Always = Excellent! Keep up the good work.

5-4 Always = Not bad, but you're probably hiring some candidates who are not successful in their positions.

Less than 4 Always = Your hiring techniques need some serious work.

CHAPTER EIGHT

Orientation: The Foundation of Customer Service

Let's assume it's a perfect world and you found four people you believe will make wonderful employees. You are convinced they will enhance your customer service program and contribute positively to your bottom line. Four months later, in this wonderful world, three out of four have quit and, worse, one is now working across the street for the competition!

How could this happen? The new hires were carefully interviewed, and perhaps you did everything suggested in Chapter Seven to ensure that a good hiring process was in place. Now you have a real problem; you may have to hire the first person to walk through the door.

The only good news is that you are not alone. You, like many others, have probably missed a crucial step between finding the right person and their ultimate success in the job—a proper, well-designed, orientation and initial training program.

After all, there are many industries that are known for rapid turnover—for example, restaurants, hotels, building maintenance workers, retail sales, call centers and more. It is par for the job. Many industries are seasonal in nature, or use short-term interns. They often hire college students who graduate and go on to their selected careers. Companies that use a lot of teenagers also have turnover problems. Other jobs are burnout jobs, as in a complaint call center where people can take only so much and then leave.

One of the most important foundations of good customer service is an exceptional orientation and training program, so you can bring new people up to speed quickly and make them feel comfortable in their new job. The orientation and initial training program serves four critical areas:

- Communicates to the employee the duties of the job

- Communicates how to accomplish them

- Communicates the culture of service of the organization

- Hopefully reduces turnover

Any employee orientation and training must **begin** the process of building the specific skills necessary to carry out the job duties and to help the employee understand they are **not** expected to do this overnight. A good orientation program contains the following five steps:

Step One: Ask Yourself These Questions:

- Do you rush new employees into the job and tell them, "You'll learn it as you go along?"

- Do you just throw them up against the wall and hope they stick?

- Are you guilty of the same old boring orientation of a tour of the facilities, a discussion of benefits and a video about the company that turns them off rather than on?

- Do you overload them with information they soon forget?

- Is your orientation program delegated down to the human resource department and simply a one-size-fits-all effort?

If most of your answers are "yes," you are not doing the following:

- Spending the necessary time integrating new hires into your environment.

- Giving every new employee the skills and knowledge they will need to be effective as quickly as possible.

Don't waste a great opportunity to use the orientation process as the first step in indoctrinating the new hire with your company's philosophy and culture of customer service. This step will help the employee see that you are serious when you talk about the importance of customer service.

The Wedgewood Hotel, a small boutique hotel based in Vancouver, Canada, uses their orientation program to help the new hire "clearly understand the philosophy and definition of service excellence of the hotel." They talk about overwhelming the guest with hospitality, and they discuss ways that each employee can do that in their job. This is very important because the hotel holds the prestigious Four Diamond Property Award with Five Diamonds for Service and, therefore, must consistently deliver a very high level of service. They also distribute a staff manual that clearly outlines all situations they might encounter and specific job duties.

A good orientation program will also help your employees learn the job faster resulting in fewer mistakes the first few days on the job, a better level of customer service, higher productivity more quickly and harmonious relations with existing employees. And you will have less turnover! A confident employee will do better and thus enjoy their job more, usually staying longer.

Step Two: Understand Why a Good Orientation Program Is Not An Option.

When you make your employees feel secure and comfortable with a thorough orientation program, you actually save money in mistakes made on the job while maintaining your level of service, even though the employee delivering the service is new. And if you want to retain your employees, you have to woo them—and not just during the interview. You must also woo them during the first few weeks on the job.

As you begin this process, consider these facts about the bottom line value of an orientation program. Remember them in case you ever feel that the hard work of constructing a program may not be worth it.

- A study at Corning Glass found that new employees who went through a positive orientation program were 69 percent more likely to remain with the company three years longer than those who did not.

- A similar two-year study at Texas Instruments concluded that employees who had been carefully oriented to both the company and their jobs reached full productivity two months earlier than those who weren't.

- The accounting firm Ernst & Young's own internal study showed that new employees who go through orientation are twice as likely to remain with the company longer than two years.

- The Schwan Food Company found they increased their retention rate of home delivery employees by more than 22 percent by improving their new employee orientation and training.

- According to the Pryor Report, a negative impression of your company during the first 60-90 days of employment can lead your newest employee to look for a new job within the year.

So it is important to cement the idea during the orientation and the employee's first months on the job that he has chosen the right company.

Step Three: Getting Started.

1. **Take Time:** This cannot be emphasized enough. You will pay in the long run if you don't. Be sure to make enough time to include everything an employee needs to know to develop a comfort level with the company and be a successful employee. It may take several days because you need them in their job right away, but keep at it until you feel the employee is comfortable with the job and doing well. Remember: an employee who doesn't know her job very well will feel uneasy and usually leave faster, leaving you with another turnover problem.

2. **Personalize the Process:** Each company must personalize their orientation process to their particular circumstances and environment. A small company who occasionally hires only a few employees will need a program that is different from that of a large company with more turnover.

3. **Don't Overwhelm:** All too often an employer makes the mistake of stuffing the new hire in a room, plunking a stack of corporate policy manuals in front of him, and telling him to come out when he is through. This is a recipe for disaster and quick turnover. Again, this is a silent message to the employee about how much you care about him.

Step Four: What a Good Orientation Program Needs:

Here are some common elements of positive orientation programs. Choose the ones that work for you and your company environment.

1. **Congratulate the new hire on being chosen for the job.**

- Make her feel special and honored to be hired.

- Tell her she is going to be working for a very special company.

- Thank her for choosing your organization.

2. **Let her know you are aware of her**. Her manager should call her before orientation and send her some basic information about the company. But not a lot! Don't overwhelm her with information even before she arrives.

3. **"Pre-welcome" her.** The day before the new employee starts, call her to answer any questions. This will show that you care about her as a person and lower her anxiety level.

4. **Let others know who she is. Make her feel important.** Put up her bio on the company bulletin board several days before she is to arrive for her first day of work, so other employees will know something about her and be able to welcome her. Try to include hobbies, her background, and something unusual. Ask, "What is one thing you have done that most people don't know?" It will bring forth facts that will be fun conversation starters.

5. **Explain your traditions and culture to all new employees as part of an orientation program.** Create a short history of the company, the organization chart, your ethics and values, some of your acronyms and the common language they will hear people use. For example, NASA uses many acronyms that can be confusing to a new hire. Inform new employees about who your competitors are, who your customers are and how they are expected to treat those customers. Tell how you are different from other organizations that offer the same service or product.

- An automobile dealer has their new car salespeople sit and observe the other employees on the showroom floor for two or three days to see how they run the operation and what is unique about it. The owner emphasizes that their culture is very different from other car dealers, and it is essential that the new hires learn and understand this.

Explain that your company's most important goal is delivering exceptional service. Leaders in the company should take part in this section of the orientation. This sends a very strong message about the importance of customer service.

- A university has made some of their traditions into a game where participants match up the name of the tradition with its description. At the beginning of the orientation they have a "learning tournament." Employees read material individually and then compete for prizes when they can give the correct answer. This technique is much more effective and memorable than lecturing.

6. **Emphasize Customer Service!** Be sure to include information on your customer service philosophy. Abacus Plumbing Company puts their new plumbers through an extensive customer service course that stresses how the customer comes first in their company. They also have the new hires ride with an experienced plumber for at least a week to solidify the learning and to see how the general philosophy is put into practice.

7. **Explain your company's "unwritten rules."** There are always many of these that are helpful for your new hire to know. For instance, if your company is very informal, let the employee know that it is okay to eat at her desk or that leaving work with a clean workspace is a company expectation. Tell them about your company parties and celebrations. Does everyone bowl together once a week, or have some other activity where everyone in the company or department participates?

- A commercial real estate company includes a program on general professionalism in their orientation. It includes information on how to dress, what level of initiative they expect, the team behaviors the company wants and other issues that are not in the employee manual yet are important to the new employee's success.

8. **Mission and vision statements should be taken seriously—but use a spoonful of sugar.** Introduce new hires to your mission and/or service vision statement. But help to make it stick with a game, rather than just pasting the words up on the wall. If you have an orientation group of eight people or more, try this exercise:

Divide your orientation group into two teams and line them up on opposite sides of the room. The first person in each line is given a printed copy of the company mission or vision statement. The first person in the line reads it to the next person in line. But the second person cannot see the printed copy.

The second person then recites the statement, as much as he can remember, to the third person in line and so on until they get to the last person in line.

That last person then goes to a flip chart or a whiteboard and writes the statement as they heard it. The team with the most correct words wins a small prize. Then write the correct mission or vision statement below the one generated by each team.

9. **Cover all the legal and safety issues.** Give new employees a rundown of company rules and policies. Let them know what is cause for immediate termination (stealing, drug abuse, sexual harassment, etc.) and the policies on being late, calling in sick, etc. Cover the safety and probationary period rules. If your company has a rules and policies sheet the employee needs to sign, do it now. Make sure they understand the grievance policy.

10. **Benefits should be explained as the employee is able to use them.** For instance, if an employee's medical or dental benefits don't take effect until ninety days after they are hired, you do not need to explain that part of the benefits in the first few days or weeks of the orientation. In fact, many companies separate benefits from other parts of the orientation so as to not overwhelm the new employee.

Give information to the employee's family. It can be a welcoming letter, copies of past newsletters, if you do one, an invitation to an evening benefits explanation, or anything that will help the family support the employee in his work.

11. **Compensation issues.** Factors that affect the employee's compensation will be anxiously awaited, so cover them in the beginning of the orientation process. Clearly outline work hours, pay schedule, time card issues, salary review frequency, overtime, payroll deductions and worker compensation issues.

Step Five: Mandatory Elements of an Effective Orientation Program:

Always keep this in mind: Don't shortchange this process or you will have a high turnover rate. As mentioned before, most employees leave within the first few months if they feel frustrated and unsure about the job. Increasing the new hire's confidence about his ability to do the job will decrease turnover. Spend more time up front in the orientation and hiring process, and you will keep your employees longer. Consider these steps:

1. **Orientation to their department and its function.** Discuss what kinds of behaviors are rewarded and how. Describe company expectations of their area or department, how the work flows, and what teamwork is expected.

   - A plumbing company manager acquaints new hires with their company standards—how to keep their vehicle, how their uniform needs to look, and other aspects of what they expect from an employee. This lets them know how to behave in clear, definable terms.

   Don't gloss over the challenges of their specific job. Be honest about the difficult parts. For example, don't let them be surprised by a lot of difficult customers, or times when the workload is overwhelming. Hopefully you have already mentioned the challenges in the job interview, but go over them again. Tell them what to expect and how to handle it. Don't just throw them to the wolves. If you do, they will soon become frustrated and leave, and you will be faced with going through the whole process all over again.

2. **Orientation to the employee's specific job.** If they are servers in a restaurant, for instance, tell them specifically the time frame for greeting a guest (e.g., within two minutes of being seated), the way to present the menu and specials and other very specific behaviors expected in the job.

Keep the following in mind when conducting an orientation session:

- Don't rush it.

- Go slowly and make sure everyone understands what you are saying.

- Review the job descriptions clearly.

- Explain clearly what performance standards are used.

- Explain how their work will be evaluated.

- Describe how the person's work affects other team members, both positively and negatively.

- Discuss how their job contributes to the mission and success of the company.

While it seems obvious, take the new hire on a tour of their job area and introduce him to the staff that can help them. For example, "This is Jeff. He can help you with customer service issues. He's great at that." Use the introductions of a new employee as an opportunity to praise your current employees.

Be creative. Don't just plant him in a chair and then lecture. Some companies turn the tour into a fast-paced scavenger hunt, with the employee looking for useful items, and discovering key locations and people's names in the process. Provide job aids so he can teach himself how to use the e-mail and telephone systems in the comfort of his own job space.

Don't forget the small stuff: Other important information to cover includes rest and meal break times and places, travel policies and expense reimbursement, the smoking policy and where to go if they have a problem.

3. **Ensure that your program is working. Test the employee at the end of the orientation process.** This will make sure the information has been retained and understood. It also helps new employees acclimate and move up to speed faster while giving you one last chance to make sure you hired the right person. In one company, if the new employee doesn't pass the test, they reserve the right to terminate employment. That usually makes the new hire sit up and listen! You can do a formal test or turn it into a less-threatening game. See Appendix C for an example of a game you can use.

4. **Throw a party for their first day on the job.** You have a party when someone leaves, right? Well, it is more important to do it when someone is new in the job. Even if you can't have a party, put up a welcome sign and some balloons. Have breakfast bagels or muffins on the new employee's desk and encourage everyone to drop by to have breakfast and meet him. Make him feel welcome and introduce him to his coworkers. If possible and applicable, arrange several people to be responsible for having lunch with him during his first week on the job. Have a regional manager or some higher-level person off-site call to welcome him to the company. Include a "Welcome Aboard" note in his first paycheck, signed by someone with an impressive title.

Arrange for his desk, computer, chair, office space, phone, uniform and other supplies to be ready for him. Ensure that other employees will be available to help him with all the questions he is sure to have.

5. **Schedule a follow-up to the orientation and training in two weeks.** New employees are often overwhelmed when they are first hired and do not retain all the information conveyed in the orientation for any length of time. Plan to have a formal meeting about two weeks after the employee has been in the job. Ask, "What questions do you have now that you have been on the job a little while?" Not, "Do you have any questions?" The latter question often results in no questions because they don't want to appear dumb. Schedule future follow-ups if you feel they are necessary.

6. **Assign a supportive mentor or buddy for several months.** It will not only help the new employee over the "rough spots" during the first few months on the job; it will also give ownership and prestige to the mentor. In addition, the new employee is much more likely to be accepted by the existing employees when under the wing of a mentor.

In order to help your current employees be more enthusiastic about shepherding the new employee, who takes time from their own job, offer to pay them a little extra while they are acting as a mentor. A successful seafood restaurant, known for their high level of service, gives the mentor twenty five cents more an hour while they train and guide the new hire.

7. **Have the new hire sign a customer service pledge as part of the orientation.** This will emphasize the company's focus on the importance of customer service. When you have people sign a list of things that they will do and display it prominently, they will be more likely to actually do it. It also makes a good coaching tool when they do not exhibit the behaviors on the pledge. Chapter Eleven will discuss more about coaching for improved performance.

SAMPLE PLEDGE

At XYZ Company our customers are everything. Without them, nothing else matters. They are our paychecks and our very reason for being. We are dedicated to providing our customers with the best service.

I realize that in order to make that happen, I must be continually focused on the customer and look at all systems, procedures and interpersonal interaction with the customer in mind. I must perform my job exceptionally well for every customer, every time.

I pledge to work with my team members and do everything I can to support them so that superior customer service occurs.

I PLEDGE TO DO MY PART TO MAKE CUSTOMER SERVICE HAPPEN FOR EVERY CUSTOMER, EVERY TIME!

Signed: _____

Date: _____

8. **Make it mandatory for everybody.** Don't fall into the trap of thinking orientation is just for certain people or positions. Make it clear that everyone is to go through orientation, from vice presidents to the front-line staff. It can be designed differently for different positions, of course, but everyone needs to go through a formal orientation of some sort.

9. **Evaluate your orientation/training program regularly.** You should do this twice: once at the end of the program, and then about two months later. At this time the employee will be able to make suggestions as to what would have made his introduction to the job easier.

10. **Use this "Welcome Aboard" checklist to customize an orientation for your company or department.**

(Choose the appropriate letter from the following code and write in the spaces below. Also, decide who will be responsible for each of the elements and write that in too. Then give the new employee a copy of the list.)

D = first day

W = first week

M = first month

F = future months

_____ History and organization of the company

_____ Ethics, mission and values of the company

_____ Common language, unwritten rules and other culture issues

_____ Customers and competitors

_____ Employee philosophy

_____ Your customer service philosophy

_____ Tour of the facilities

_____ Benefits

_____ Training for their specific job

_____ Legal issues

_____ Security issues

_____ Parking

_____ Name badge and uniform

_____ Orientation to their department and function

_____ Orientation to their particular job duties

_____ On-the-job training

_____ Assignment to a mentor

_____ Follow-ups—how many? When?

_____ Evaluation of the orientation program

Remember: Employees should have knowledge of three things:

1. The company's products, services and external customers.

2. Organizational structure, culture and internal customers.

3. What the organization expects of the employee.

Beware of using the "fire hose" approach. This is where you turn on a fire hose of information and hose them down until they can't take any more. Your orientation program should be a key success factor in bringing new employees on board in such a way that they will stay longer and serve your customers well. It should not saturate or overwhelm people.

Think of it as adopting them into your company home. Besides just teaching them about the company and their job, get your new hires excited about working there. Make the experience of orientation fun and exciting. It will set the tone for their entire work experience. And if it is a good one, you will have an employee who knows their job and is excited about doing it.

A superior orientation program will set the stage for continual training. In the next chapter, we will discuss the specific elements of a training program that will continue the steps toward creating an exceptional customer service environment.

A final word: No matter how well organized and employee-driven your orientation program is, you may still find yourself losing ground with turnovers. That will be discussed more fully in Chapter Twelve, which outlines retention tactics.

CHAPTER NINE

Establishing an Effective Training Program

Your employees suffer—along with customer service and profits—when they are not well trained. Ineffective or sloppy training can be disastrous. It's almost guaranteed to lose customers, and it can have an unintended effect on employee morale. That, in turn, leads to high turnover.

Here's an example. The office supply business is currently dominated by "depot/warehouse" stores and online or catalog sales. The era of the neighborhood stationery store has pretty much ended, primarily because the chain stores can offer better volume-based prices, especially now that electronic products dominate the office market. These stores can also stock a much wider choice of products, and are especially valuable to those with home offices or small businesses who have to watch overhead costs.

One advantage of this business trend, especially for small business owners, is the ability to bring graphic and design work in-house. Practically any young employee today can use one of the variety of page-making or brochure design programs and many of the older generation have been smart enough to keep up and learn the programs too.

After receiving a $2000 estimate from a graphic artist, Bob taught himself how to use a program that allows him to make business cards, marketing materials and press releases. He had no doubt his work would be less *snappy*, but saving $2000 and learning a new skill is worth considering.

All Bob needed was coated paper, and heavy business card paper. It seemed simple, but after 15 minutes in his local warehouse store, he was ready to tear his hair out. He brought a list, and three consecutive employees, all wearing badges that read "Customer Experience Associate," sent him to the paper department. However, the "Customer Experience Associate" for that department was somewhere else at the time. When the right employee was finally located, he informed Bob that the store did not carry what he wanted. Bob was astonished, and after the employee wandered off, he began searching the paper department himself. Naturally, he found exactly what he needed.

The customer service lesson is not that Bob was angry and vowed never to shop there again. That would mean he'd have to go to the other side of town. The moral is that, while the employee had been nice enough, he missed out on the bonus commission that he'd have earned from Bob's purchase and future purchases. This was the result of a serious lack of training. The employee in charge of the department had no idea about what was stocked in his own department.

Another customer walked up to a rental car counter. He was clearly in a hurry, but as it turned out, luck was not on his side. He drew a rental agent on her first day on the job. It was soon clear that she was not adequately trained. She didn't know how to work the computer system, and she wasn't familiar with the different vehicles offered and the features and advantages of each. She had to ask the agent standing next to her, who was waiting on another customer, how to complete each step in the rental process.

As the customer fumed and looked at his watch, the employee became even more nervous and slowed the process further. Of course, that infuriated the impatient customer further, and he snapped, "Can't you see I'm in a hurry?" The new agent, on the verge of tears, could only manage, "Well, I'm doing the best I can...".

The result was predictable. Thirty seconds later the customer stormed out the door, loudly vowing never to rent a car from that car rental agency again. Further damage was done because it occurred in front of several other customers, all equally in a hurry. The new agent was humiliated and probably not a candidate for long-term employment. The incident was not her fault. She was simply not trained properly and put on the front line before she was ready. It would have been better to operate shorthanded until she was properly trained.

Could this happen in your business? Can the absence of a good training program compromise your customer service AND harm your employees' chances of success, thereby affecting your retention rate? Do you believe that serious job training is just for the "big boys?"

Effective job training is a crucial building block of competitive-edge service. Every company **must** offer their employees training, from the initial training at orientation to ongoing development. It is especially important if you hire mostly teenage or minimum-wage workers.

Training Pays Off in Multiple Ways:

Few can disagree that training new employees before they are allowed to serve new customers is cost effective, reduces turnover and absenteeism, prevents costly errors and eliminates possible causes of customer dissatisfaction. But if you are hoping that workers will turn up on the company doorstep already trained by former employers, forget it. That just doesn't happen.

You must offer training and retraining. Frequent, continual training has been shown to reduce pilfering, time-cheating and other petty crimes against the company. Loyalty and commitment to the company flourishes when workers are well trained.

Above all, the quality of the training is what will distinguish your business and your employees from all others. "Training is paramount to everything," says Kenneth Goode, President and owner of Goode Air Conditioning and Heating. He strongly believes this and puts his resources behind his philosophy.

Goode sends his people to the technical schools offered by his vendors like Trane and Lennox. Even though it will cost $3000 to send his people through these courses, he feels it is critical to maintaining excellent customer service.

Beyond this, Goode also conducts weekly breakfast meetings where employees discuss problems, remedies, and procedures and learn from each other. He also trains by passing on articles he thinks would be informative to his people from the numerous periodicals he reads that are related to his field.

Any employer has to realize that customer service is emotional labor. It is very draining to deal with people all day and to be continually positive. Frequent training can keep them giving good service to every customer, every time. Beware of using the sink or swim method by throwing the employee into the job with minimal training and hoping they will learn on the job.

Small businesses can have effective training, but they may have to be creative.

If you are a small business owner, it is likely that orientation and the first training will take place on the employee's first day of work, because you have to get them up and running as soon as possible. Larger companies often have the luxury of training gradually over a longer period of time, because there are more existing employees to do the job until the new hire can get up to speed.

But if you don't have a training department or a big budget, don't despair. You just have to get creative. Martha Justice, President of The Premier Company, a printing, direct mail and fulfillment organization, has developed some innovative ways to train her employees.

First, she uses her suppliers to provide information that will help them in their jobs. For instance, she might invite a paper supplier to come in and help her employees learn more about the intricacies of paper. Or she will invite UPS to explain some of their shipping procedures and how they fit into the employees' jobs. She also encourages employees to read a book and share information with the rest of the staff. "It's a struggle when you're small and have no-or a low-training budget, so you have to get creative," Justice says.

Paige Reid, Training Manager of A&E—The Graphics Complex, puts all new hires though a training orientation that involves a tour of the facility and shares an overview of the history of the business and of all the services they offer.

"Then we do a lot of one-on-one training," she says. Especially if the new hire does not have the technical skills necessary to do the job. In a classroom setting, they work on every aspect of the job and then use experts in their future departments to fill in any gaps.

After new employees are on the job for thirty days, they do an observation test to see if they need more training and also create two-hour training modules for manager's and assistant manager's meetings. They deliver segments on the importance of documentation, how to develop employees, team building and other information to help the employees perform their jobs better.

It's vital for your employees to know more than just their own universe. Once hired, it is up to you to provide the kind of training that will enable them to do things right the first time and thereafter. Train them in their own job and also cross-train for others, so they will have an overview of the whole process. When employees are cross-trained, they know how the entire service process flows, and this will increase their abilities to solve customer service problems on their own.

Cross-training also avoids the situations where every deviation from the rules or normal procedures calls for manager intervention. While you can't let everyone have total control over customer interactions, you can give them some wide parameters within which to solve problems. For example, you could give them a dollar amount they are allowed to use to keep the customer happy. Within that amount, they can do what they think is right.

Avoid the "knee jerk" reaction of ordering training only when people are caught doing something wrong. Don't be the CEO of a business who calls his company, receives terrible telephone service and immediately orders the head of training to send everyone who answers the telephone through a telephone etiquette program. It's much better to offer this training **before** the problem occurs.

Prevent future headaches. Hire the right people to begin with, take the time to orient them correctly, maintain a supportive atmosphere throughout the company, occasionally check the service levels of your people and have an ongoing program of listening and adjusting to customer feedback. Then there will be no need for a hastily called training session because of a lack of customer service skills.

Who to Train and for What Goal?

Don't make the mistake of thinking that training in customer service is only for the front-line people who have actual contact with customers. As mentioned in a previous chapter, all customer service efforts must first come from the top, and so must the training initiatives.

Your training programs should take place on four levels:

1. **Administration and executives** should learn their role in achieving competitive-edge customer service. They should be trained in the overall vision and actions needed in establishing and reinforcing the culture of service. Things like establishing the service strategy and vision and setting goals in customer service levels are important first steps we have already discussed.

Then they need to model the customer friendly behaviors they expect from their employees. They cannot call a pep rally meeting and toot the horn for customer service and then turn around and not be available to their customers.

An owner and CEO of a supply company was asked by his sales and customer service manager to accompany him on some calls to get customer feedback. The CEO refused, saying that it was the job of sales and customer service to do that.

Wrong! He, of all people, must show a willingness to listen to his customers and to find out what needs to be changed. That is more powerful than all the slogans about customer service.

2. **Mangers and supervisors** need training in how to make the customer service goals a reality and forge a team all working toward the same service goals. In other words, they must exemplify how to manage the process and create the motivation to make it happen. They need to understand that one of their roles is to support the customer contact people and remove barriers to delivering exceptional customer service.

They need training in coaching and counseling their people to better performance. They also need to attend all of their employees' training sessions so they know what behaviors have been taught. Only then will they know what behaviors the employees should be expected to exhibit. Don't just "send your people to a training class" and plan to fix poor service that way. Managers must take a very active role if they expect the training to "take."

A manager of a medical clinic is famous with his employees for walking around his business asking, "What one thing keeps you from doing your job well?" If it is a system or procedure, he fixes it. If it is a lack of knowledge, he arranges for more training. After all, who knows better than the front line people where things are breaking down?

3. **Front line customer contact people** need to learn their roles and the skills of dealing with customers on a daily basis. Listening skills, problem solving, handling angry customers and personal stress management are some of the skills that customer service representatives need on a daily basis. They need to learn the attitude that "The customer is my paycheck" and that providing exceptional service to their customers is their reason for being in business.

4. **Everyone else in the company** should be trained in customer service awareness and servicing their internal customers. They may never see an actual customer face-to-face, but serve those who do. They need to realize that "Anyone who needs something from me in order to get their job done is my customer."

So the payroll department's customers are everyone in the company. Without an accurate paycheck on a regular basis, there will be many unhappy employees who may take it out on the customers.

On-the-Job Training Needs Special Talents.

After the initial training, you often need to add on-the-job training. Be sure the trainer you choose is well qualified. Some people are naturally good teachers; others are not. Often the training is conducted by a harried line manager who doesn't have the time, resources or the know-how to do it properly.

Or you can use the "Sit with Sally" technique. A new employee finds out about the job by sitting with or following another employee around. Learning by example can be a very effective form of training and one that will solidify your culture of service by learning from someone who believes in and demonstrates your company's culture of service.

But make sure they are willing to train. Some people do not want the hassles or responsibility of training. Often they are so busy themselves they will not have the time to do it properly. Paying an on-the-job trainer a financial incentive during the training period can also make them more eager to take the time to do it.

Before training begins, be sure to:

- Break the job into small bite-sized pieces or tasks.

- Determine the skills needed to do these tasks.

- Define the minimum performance level.

- Set a time limit for reaching each level of skill.

When you are ready to actually lead the training session, follow this five-step process:

1. Explain in detail how the task is performed. It is good to have this written down so the trainee can follow along. They can use this job aid when they are asked to perform the job by themselves.

2. Show the employee the correct way to do the task.

3. As you watch, have the employee perform the skill.

4. Critique the performance, being sure to praise what they have done right.

5. Repeat the process until they do it right.

Martha Justice, mentioned previously, does on-the-job training. When she hires a new employee, she has them work in each department for a little while to get a good overview of the company. The new employee learns the database department, the prepress and art departments and even the pressroom. "Learning the entire process helps employees serve customers better," Justice says.

Areas of Training

Training begins by knowing the behaviors and actions that produce enthusiastic customers. That's why listening to your customers, as discussed in a previous chapter, is so important. It is from this activity alone that you will know where to direct your training.

There are two general areas in which to provide training:

1. Technical skills

2. Behavioral skills

Companies that produce superior service strike a balance between training in both of these skills. Have you ever dealt with a clerk who was very friendly and accommodating but didn't know the technical attributes of his merchandise? Think of the last time you purchased some electronic equipment. Was the sales clerk able to explain all the different features of the various products and how they differed? If not, it was probably because he wasn't trained well enough to start with or continually trained on the new merchandise as it came in.

Technical skills training covers features of the products or service, details of physically performing the job correctly and development of all required skills. This training enables the employee to do the job and prevents frustration and feelings of inadequacy. It also prevents the mistakes that result in angry customers.

For instance, computer skills are necessary in most jobs today, yet many companies change the software overnight and then hand the employee a manual and expect them to learn by themselves. Then they wonder why so many mistakes are made.

New employees also need to be familiar with all the paperwork that will be required of them. They should be taught how to complete it correctly, why they're filling it out, how the information will be used and who uses it. This goes back to the idea that the more your customer service representatives know about the process, the more they can troubleshoot when problems arise.

Technical skills training teaches how to fry the French fries at exactly the right temperature or how to write a travel itinerary. Restaurants need to teach employees how to set the table perfectly every time. Training teaches the machine operator how to operate the machinery efficiently and safely. Refresher technical skills training may also be necessary when jobs change or when new products, procedures or a new telephone system is introduced.

If you don't continually train your employees on all aspects of your product or service, they will never be able to answer your customer's needs. Resist the urge to throw your people on the front line without thoroughly teaching your employees everything they need to know in this area. If you don't, the result will be unhappy customers who will take their business elsewhere. Can you afford that?

Behavioral skills training is a term that describes a broad range of skills in which you cannot set exact ways and procedures. It focuses on the skills and attitudes needed to deal with people. For example, the importance of a sincere smile, active listening, adept handling of difficult customers and other "people skills" are all behaviors that every employee needs. Of course, you can teach employees to welcome each customer with a smile and "How may I help you?" You can teach them to say, "Thank you for shopping at Megamart." But your training must go further than that or you will end up with employees who act like robots.

Behavioral training helps to establish a culture of service in your organization that purports the customer is the reason the whole company exists. All too often employees forget this and think their job is keeping the shelves stocked or the data in the right column. They lose sight of the real reason they are performing their jobs.

A successful training program integrates both of these areas. Avoid training solely in technical skills and bringing your people back later for the interpersonal, behavioral side. Both skills must be taught together in order to turn out a successful customer service representative.

Costs of Not Training

Steve Lauer and B. Jack Gebhardt, in their book, *Now Hiring! Finding and Keeping Good Help for Your Entry-Wage Jobs*, maintain that for every hour up front that you skimp on training a new employee, you can expect to devote two to three hours, minimum, fixing goof-ups down the line. They go on to say, "For every employee you fail to train well, you can expect three to five phone calls at home to fix the problems and uncertainties of these poorly trained employees."

So taking the time to train an employee well is not optional. It is a necessity to reach your goal of delivering such exceptional service that it becomes your competitive edge.

Customer Service Ratings Worksheet

Rate your customer service representatives with excellent, good or poor.

1. Job knowledge. Understands products, services and customer service procedures. They don't have to ask someone down the hall how to do it or look it up in a procedure manual while the customer is waiting.

   Excellent Good Poor

2. Motivation to serve customers. Really likes to serve customers and shows it in his attitude.

   Excellent Good Poor

3. Work ethic. Constantly strives to maintain high standards of customer service.

   Excellent Good Poor

4. Energy and body language. Remains alert and attentive and works with an enthusiastic energy level.

   Excellent Good Poor

5. Flexibility. Is able to change her service style based on customer needs and desires.

   Excellent Good Poor

6. Able to deal with unhappy customers well. Is able to take customer's anger professionally, not personally.

   Excellent Good Poor

7. Follow up. Delivers on promises and commitments made to customers.

   Excellent Good Poor

8. Initiative. Is able to go beyond what is normally done in a situation. Constantly looks for ways to surprise and delight your customers.

   Excellent Good Poor

Obviously, all "excellent" ratings are the goal here. If you weren't able to do that, look at your training programs to see where you need to improve. Or go back even further to the hiring and orientation process. The problem may lie there.

But training alone won't cause exceptional customer service to happen. It is a very important piece of the puzzle, yes, but not the only one. Now the motivation piece must be put in place. The next chapter will show how you can create a climate of motivation for your employees so they will want to consistently deliver superior service.

CHAPTER TEN

Creating a Climate of Motivation

Motivating employees, especially when customer service is part of their job, often requires a manager who is part social worker, part cheerleader, part judge (and jury), as well as someone who understands the company's customer base well enough to know how an employee can most please them.

To keep your employees fired-up and motivated means maintaining an environment of motivation at all times. If you are not doing this in your company, you can never hope to achieve a level of superior service that will give you the competitive edge. Unmotivated employees are not capable of exceptional customer service.

Notice that we say you should create a climate of motivation. Not simply "to motivate your employees." Your employees are already motivated. They are motivated to do what they want to do. To work in their comfort zone. If you want to move them out of their comfort zone, you must give them a reason to do it.

Orientation and continual training teaches your employees **what** they should do, but how do you create the **"want to"** factor? How do you get them to serve the customer well every time even if a supervisor is not looking? How do you get them to give you discretionary effort? That is, how do you get the extra effort that will raise your customer service from ordinary to extraordinary and serve as your competitive edge?

A customer in a grocery store was picking over some packages of strawberries, but couldn't find anything he wanted to buy. As he turned to leave and go to a rival grocery store, a young stock boy wheeled up a cart full of strawberries that had just been delivered. "Here's a new batch," he said. "See if you can find something you like in here." He had noticed that the customer had not picked up any strawberries and had gone to the back to see what he could find. That is discretionary effort and a signal that a customer service culture is deeply embedded in the organization and that the stocker was motivated to please the customer.

The more contact with customers that your employees have, the more motivation they need. As mentioned before, dealing with customers is often described as "emotional labor" because it is a constant drain on your emotions, which can be very tiring. Customer service reps can never have a down day. They must always be smiling and be "on" no matter what their personal circumstances. That can be difficult to do.

That is why creating a climate of motivation for your employees is a key to not only retaining them, but also having them serve your customers the way you want them served. If that climate is not present, sabotage of your customer service efforts can often result, inter-personal conflicts escalate and the customer is lost in the shuffle. No information on improving customer service will be forthcoming from your front line. They will do just the bare minimum and that's it.

Creating a climate of motivation is a complex issue with many parts that must be in place. It is much more than beer blasts and casual day. It is not about slogans. It is not calling in a motivational speaker and expecting your employees to magically become motivated. Those could be parts of creating a climate of motivation, but just small parts. Many other types of motivators must be present in your workplace.

Motivation Starts with the Manager.

The main person responsible for motivation is the employee's manager. It must be the most important part of a manager's job if you want the kind of employees that deliver exceptional service without having to be told everything they must do. This kind of employee "gets it," and is constantly looking for ways to surprise and delight his customer.

In companies that are most successful in delivering exceptional service, the managers are present as much as possible. You cannot always hole up in your office and expect your employees to deliver the best service possible. The more you are visible, the better your service will be. But you can't always do that, so use some of these techniques to create a climate of motivation for when you cannot be present.

Start by asking your employees what motivates them. This is so simple, yet few managers take time to discover this. Gather your team together and ask them what motivates them. Then ask them to rank-order the list. Next, ask what demotivates them. Don't assume you have no demotivators in your workplace. Chances are you have several. More will be discussed on this subject later.

Don't accept a paycheck or money as the answer. Most employees will give that one first. Dig deeper to find out what other things they are getting from the job. Money as a motivator is quite low on every list of research done on this subject.

Steve Bates, writing in HR magazine, quotes Robert Heneman, Professor of Management and Human Relations at Ohio State University, saying "Research shows that you need a 7 percent or 8 percent compensation increase just to catch anyone's attention. Anything below that is welcome but doesn't lead to significantly greater effort on the part of the employee to drive business results."

Not that money can't be used in your reward and recognition process. It can. It just can't be the only element.

Generally, there are two types of motivators: external and internal. Use each of these in the process of creating a climate of motivation.

External motivators can include rewards, incentives, bonuses, recognition and praise.

Internal motivators are feelings of competence and accomplishment in the job, being valued, feeling that what they do matters, interest in the job itself, feeling they have a measure of control over how the job is done and pride in the job and company. A good motivational climate includes both internal and external factors.

External Motivators

Rewards

There are basically three kinds of rewards:

1. "If you...then..."rewards.

These are rewards that are promised and awarded for achieving a specific goal. "If this happens, then you will be rewarded this way." It can be a decrease in the number of complaints received, exemplary attendance or safety, a lowering of the number of mistakes in customers' orders, etc.

"If you...then..." rewards can be a formal awards banquet, a party or something fun, like the manager having to wear her pajamas to work one day. It can be an extra vacation day or a few hours of time off. Some companies make it fun by having their managers make and serve a lunch to their employees upon reaching a certain customer service goal.

Century Maintenance Supply Inc. uses a PRIDE Program (Personal Responsibility In Delivering Excellence) in a variety of motivational ways. For instance, the driver PRIDE program recognizes delivery excellence by paying cash bonuses to the drivers.

2. **Instant rewards.** These are rewards that are promised and handed out right after the behavior occurs. It stems from the "catch them doing something right" method of managing and motivation. Praise, a small token award or rewards that employees give each other are examples.

Buy a bunch of fun stickers, and every time someone does something good, give them a sticker. You will be surprised at how well this is received.

You can also adapt this type of award to encourage internal customer service. (Service employees give to one another.) A dental office has an internal customer service award program called "drops in the bucket." A bucket is placed in the employee break room, and each employee is given several pieces of paper cut in the shape of drops of water. When an employee receives some special internal customer service from one of her co-workers, she writes the employee's name and specifics of the action on the "drop of water," and gives it to the employee who then places it in the bucket. At the end of each week, several drops are pulled and gift certificates to a local restaurant are awarded.

Rice University's Fondren Library has an "owlet" award based on the school's mascot of an owl. Employees write a short note to other employees when they have done something special for them. In e-mail, Sara Lowman, the library director, lists each recipient of an owlet note and why they have received the award.

3. **Surprise awards.** These are awards that are totally unexpected and are often combined with an instant style of delivery. When your department achieves something special in the way of customer service that is unexpected, treat them to a surprise lunch. If you observe someone going the extra mile, give the employee two movie passes.

Quest Business Agency, a privately held company that specializes in business-to-business marketing and communication programs, surprised one employee by naming her a "research goddess" on the employee's tenth work anniversary. Everyone at the party dressed in togas and they snuck her family in to participate in the ceremony. This is certainly a more memorable celebration and more motivating than the usual service pin.

A hotel banquet manager surprised the banquet staff with pizza after serving a particularly difficult lunch group. If applicable, it can be something like going home early or taking an extra break.

When you are running shorthanded and someone really pitches in, give them a Nestle Crunch bar with a note saying, "Thanks for helping out in a crunch."

Every week, pick a "mystery manager" and give that person five silver dollars. During the week, as the manager interacts with the employees, she asks what they have done to reach the company's customer service goals. If they can tell the manager at least one thing, award them a silver dollar.

Have a "surprise treat day" once a month to let employees know you appreciate them. Rent a popcorn machine or serve everyone coffee and donuts. Vary the surprise.

Avoid "Employee of the Month" awards because they result in only one winner. Try to make the awards achievable by everyone. For instance, an attendance award, which is very important in keeping your level of service high, can be attained by every employee. If you employ mystery shopping to measure service levels, you can tie rewards to that. When a customer "shops" an employee to rate the level of service received and it is high, post the results in a public place and reward the employee in some way.

Make the rewards:

Fair = available to every employee

Fun = capture their attention and make them want to try for the award

Of value = something that fits their wants and needs

Recognition

The American Management Association conducted a study with 6000 participants across the USA.

The survey had only two questions:

1. Do you get enough recognition at work?

2. Would you do a better job if you got more recognition?

To number one, 97 percent of the respondents said "no." To number two, 98 percent said "yes." Yet many managers think they don't have time to give recognition or that it won't make any difference.

Many different and continual forms of recognition must be present in your organization in order to create that climate of motivation that will help your employees give the best customer service possible.

There are three forms of employee recognition:

1. Work Recognition

- More challenging assignments that help them grow

- Promotions

- Increased control over resources

- More decision authority

- Special development projects

- More money and control for their budget

- Cross training

2. Verbal Recognition

- Praise

- Recognition

- Letters or some form of written praise

- Award events, serious and funny

- Celebration luncheons/activities

- Taking an interest in the employee/listening to them

3. Things

- Monetary rewards

- Trophies/plaques

- Certificates

- Special achievement clubs

- Rewards of special interest to the individual employee

- Tickets/dinners/trips

Decide which ones will work in your environment and use them on a regular basis. Change them up every once in a while, because they grow old fast and no longer act as motivators. Recognition and reward programs must be changed frequently in order to be effective.

Include Lots of Praise.

Be sure to include praise in your motivation program. Everyone needs that.

It is one of the most powerful motivators and recognition tools there is and costs nothing but a little time. The US Army found that praise works better than criticism to get soldiers to do a better job. When soldiers were praised for their efforts, 9 out of 10 did a better job the next time around, but only 3 out of 10 did a better job when criticized.

Be sure that you are giving effective praise, however. If the receiver doesn't trust the praisegiver's motives or the person praises too lavishly or too often, it will backfire and become a demotivator.

Praise can also be given in the wrong place. Some people like it in public; others want it quietly, behind the scenes. Co-workers may become jealous if one or two workers get all the praise. Find out which of your employees prefer to be recognized in public and which prefer to be recognized in private. Each of your employees will be different. This kind of behavior will help raise your employee's self-esteem, and they will be more likely to give you that discretionary effort that translates into exceptional customer service. People are motivated to perform at a level consistent with their perceptions of self-competency.

Every one of your employees is doing something right. Notice what it is and praise them for it, even if there are other things you wish they would do better. Focusing on their strengths rather than their weaknesses will help you get the most of your employees. When you discover their strengths, try to find a job for them that utilizes those strengths.

One manager found that his IT manager was really good at dealing with people and wanted a job with more positive people contact. He transferred him to another department where he could use the skills he preferred, thus keeping the employee and allowing him to become even better in his job.

Don't be guilty of not spending enough time with your employees to see the things they are doing right so that you can praise them. A manager of a payroll department spent all her time buried in her office doing paperwork. She rarely went out into the department to see and praise her employees. Is it any wonder that she felt she had "unmotivated workers?"

Always be specific with your praise. Don't say, "You are doing a good job." Tell the employee exactly what she is doing that makes you feel she is doing a good job. For instance, maybe she rarely takes sick days. Praise that specifically.

Often customer service managers expect every employee to give their best every day as part of their employment. After all, they are getting a paycheck, so they should be working at their best. Right? But things don't always work that way. Even multimillion-dollar sports stars need lots of praise and encouragement in order to help them play their best.

You also want to praise people with just average abilities, not just your super-stars. This will help raise their level of motivation and self-esteem and result in better performance. For instance, can you praise their consistency? If they always come to work on time, that is important. After all, if you have late employees, it is hard to deliver superior service.

Don't think you are too busy to praise. It only takes 30 seconds. Here's something you can do to help remind you to praise often. Put 10 pennies in one pocket at the beginning of the shift or workday. Then, every time you praise someone, shift one of those pennies to the other pocket. By the end of the day you should have moved all ten pennies to the other pocket.

Or get yourself a "praise pad." Select a brightly colored pad of sticky notes, and every time you see your employees do something praise-worthy, write a short note and stick it in their work area or give it to them right on the spot.

Praise must be immediate to be effective. Don't wait for a week to praise the employee. Reward them as soon as possible because you want to reinforce the link between what they have done (come in on time or shown some initiative) and the resulting praise.

Write a letter and put it in their employee file and give them a copy. Or send a letter of praise to their family or spouse about what a wonderful job they are doing.

Some managers feel that if they praise too much, the employee will slack off. Sometimes this does happen. In this case, you will need to coach the employee that the positive behavior must be continued or you will have to take disciplinary action. We will discuss more of that in the next chapter.

Other managers have such perfectionist standards that no one can ever match up to their ideals. Employees have to excel in order to win their praise. Doing just a little better than before doesn't cut it. This creates unmotivated employees who will soon leave or do just enough work to not get fired.

Steve Lauer and B. Jack Gebhardt, in their book, *Now Hiring! Finding and Keeping Good Help for Your Entry-Wage Jobs,* say, "Typically employees perform approximately 95 percent of their responsibilities in a correct or appropriate manner. And yet typically 70 to 80 percent of the feedback they receive is negative."

Remember that praise works best in a basically healthy organizational environment. It is not a substitute for fair pay and decent treatment. That is why, as discussed in this book, all the pieces of the puzzle need to be in place for superior customer service to occur.

So resolve to start praising more right now. Never underestimate the power of praise. There is a direct link between your climate of motivation and how customer friendly your employees are. It can be the extra mile that results in a service level that becomes your competitive edge.

Other Reward and Recognition Ideas.

Besides praise, there are many other things you can do to recognize and reward employees.

Create opportunities for your customers to praise your employees. Use customer surveys or reaction cards with a space for the customer to list the employee's name. A major hotel chain does this. One caveat, however: some employees may abuse the program by pestering customers to fill out a positive card. Monitor the process to make sure that doesn't happen.

Don't forget your internal customers—especially those who don't have direct contact with the customers but who support the people who do. Bestow an award called "We count on you" to tout the accomplishments of the support people who make the service to the ultimate customer possible.

Remember that rewards and recognition are not "one size fits all." This is especially true for entry level or front-line people working at the bottom of the pay scale. Have a varied menu of awards that can be customized to the individual. Then change them often to keep people interested and motivated to try to win them. Because no matter how good a program is, it will get old over time.

Here are some ideas to help you develop your own reward and recognition program.

- The "You Done Good" or "Pat on the Back" Awards.

- A free soda/snack food.

- "Great Job" cards you give out when an employee has delivered exceptional service or handled an unhappy customer well.

- Pass around a trophy. It can be awarded for some aspect of good customer service.

- Schedule a day in honor of the person or team.

- Create a Hall of Fame wall where people who have delivered superior service have their pictures posted for a month.

- Create a "yearbook" that contains everybody's photo and his or her best service achievement of the year.

- Write five or more sticky notes thanking the person for a job well done and hide them among the work on his/her desk or work area.

- When employees work extra hours that keep them away from home, send a thank you or small gift to the family members.

- Buy lunch for the worker and two to three coworkers of their choice.

- The "Life Saver" award—a dozen packs of Life Saver candies and a gift certificate—says, "Thanks for being a lifesaver."

- Reprint praise letters or verbal comments in the company newsletter or post on the bulletin board. Have a special newsletter just for customer service stories. Call it the "Extra Milers."

- Have upper management take them to lunch and listen to their ideas for improvement.

- Give them an extra break.

- Give them a two-hour lunch—and pay for dessert.

- Give a day off or cover for them on their shift for an hour or two.

- Give a lottery ticket with a note that says, "I never gamble when I count on you."

- Throw "ice-cream socials" where managers make and serve sundaes to their employees.

- Laugh-a-Day challenge—for one month each employee tries to make coworkers laugh each day with cartoons and jokes—winners receive a prize.

- Have a surprise picnic in the parking lot.

- Give employees ten-minute "joy breaks," during which they can have fun. A marshmallow fight is a good energizer.

- Favorite work—give them more of the work you know they enjoy.

- Provide personal growth opportunities like seminars.

- Develop a behind-the-scenes award specifically for those who don't deal directly with customers but whose actions support those who do.

- The "snooze" or "cruise" award. Let them come to work a half-hour later than normal or leave a half-hour earlier.

- Give movie tickets.

- Award a savings bond.

- Give a certificate good for a free housecleaning.

- Give a gift certificate to a local grocery store.

- Pay one telephone bill.

- Arrange visits to vendors.

- Provide recognition in the newsletter or on a "Celebration" bulletin board.

- Schedule a day in honor of the person or team. Make them Queen or King for the day.

- For Thanksgiving, write each of your staff a "Thank You" note telling how thankful you are they are working for you. Personalize each one.

- Make the celebration of customer service week a big deal.

- Send a welcome note to new employees.

- Have a WOW award.

John B. Moore Company, a home services company, uses gold stars in their recognition program. Employees who have met their weekly goals are awarded a gold star, and their name is posted in the technician's meeting room.

Foleys Department stores also has a gold-star system. They have a friendliness

Customer Service: How to Do It Right!

program where employees are mystery shopped and rated on their degree of friendliness, and when they score high, they are awarded a gold star. Accumulating several of them gives a person a diamond star, which is then rewarded with an invitation to a special recognition banquet.

Don't forget, however, if your employees don't value the reward or recognition, they won't work hard for something they don't want.

A manager in an insurance firm decided to have a customer service contest where the prize would be a mountain bike. The only problem, however, was that only two employees out of 25 would be interested in a mountain bike. The employees were so turned off by the prize that the customer service ratings actually went down instead of up.

Internal Motivators

When you practice the external motivators above, you are also creating some of the elements that will lay the groundwork for internal motivation. For instance, when you praise employees often, you will help to create a feeling of competence in the job. And when people feel they are good at what they do, they will strive even more.

Here are some things that will contribute to internal motivation in your employees.

1. **A sense of competence** is one important internal motivator. When an employee feels that he is good at his job, it gives him a sense of self-esteem and worth that shows itself in better job performance. But when employees have a lack of confidence, they will perform less effectively.

    Lack of a feeling of competence is a pervasive motivation problem, especially if a lot of your employees are young. That's why training them well before allowing them to serve customers, making the workload reasonable and communicating realistic performance expectations are important. If that doesn't happen, demotivation will occur.

    Be sure you continually give your employees the skills they need to feel competent. For instance, many younger employees (and some more mature ones) do not know how to handle angry customers. They end up taking it personally and escalating the conflict until they have driven the customer out the door muttering that they will never do business with you again. That will result in the employee feeling bad about the incident and doubting their competence in dealing with customers.

Coaching your employees to improve performance is a critical way to help them improve their job skills and therefore their sense of competence. Coaching techniques will be discussed in the next chapter.

2. **Assure their work is meaningful to them.** They must get a sense of satisfaction from the work and use their full range of skills. They must have an interest in what they are doing. Have you asked your employees what they like about their work? What makes them excited? Finding their internal motivators by asking or observing is the first step in creating the "want to" factor.

3. **Give them responsibility for the results they produce**, not just the work. As much as possible, let them decide how they are going to do the job. Of course in some industries, like the fast-food area, there are lots of procedures to follow. But give them as many options as you can.

Solicit and listen to your employees' ideas on how to improve service. Put some of the responsibility on the employees for finding systems and procedures to help improve your service. Even if you will not be able to implement an idea, thank them for the effort, and explain why it cannot be used.

All of these things will result in a good work relationship with their manager, another key to internal motivation. More employees leave because of a poor manager than because of poor pay.

Demotivators

You can have all of the above motivators in place, but if you don't also eliminate demotivators, nothing will work. You will continue to have low morale and motivation and, therefore, poor customer service. Are you guilty of any of these?

- **Rewarding the wrong things.** When you say that you want behavior that pleases your customers, and then give raises and promotions to those who push through the greatest number of customers no matter what kind of service they deliver, you will be creating a demotivating atmosphere.

Customer Service: How to Do It Right!

A company that specializes in fast oil changes and other car maintenance preaches that pleasing the customer is the most important thing. But what they reward is car counts—how many cars they push through the process. Sometimes this causes customers to feel rushed with their concerns and ignored in the quest for speed. Does this result in superior service? No. It results in customers feeling that they are just a number.

- **Signaling right and turning left.** When you say that your company goal is to always put the customer first and then formulate rules or policies that make it hard to do this, you are creating a big demotivator.

A grocery store, part of a nationwide chain, decided to run their inventory lean because of an economic downturn. But that meant customers would not always be able to buy the product they wanted. The store was frequently running out of staples like milk and orange juice.

When a customer asked an employee taking inventory why they were out of a product, he seemed confused about how to react. "If we are to always put the customer first, why am I being forced to run such a low inventory that the customer can't find what they want?" he asked.

- **Unnecessary rules, processes and systems.** When you have rules and regulations for reasons that employees don't understand, they will act as barriers to achieving excellent customer service. The same goes for systems and processes that make the work more difficult. Ask your people what takes too long, what keeps them from doing their best work possible, and other things that serve to create a climate of demotivation.

Yes. It is important for employees to follow your policies and procedures. But often there are too many and they have not been adequately explained to employees. So when a customer is told of a policy and asks "why," all the employee knows to say is "I dunno. They just tell me to do it." Obviously, this does not result in the customer leaving with a warm fuzzy feeling about your company.

- **Office politics.** If the perception is that, in order to succeed, you must butter up the boss or concentrate on politics instead of performance, your employees will become demotivated and either leave or spend all their time playing politics.

- **Constant change.** Some change is good and very necessary to stay competitive today. But if changes consist of constant downsizing, reorganization or reengineering, employees will quickly turn off their discretionary efforts, and do just what is necessary to complete the job.

A call center is now going through their fourth downsizing in two years. Employees never know if they will have a job the next day, so they have hunkered down and are just holding their breath until it is their turn. A lot of time that could be spent serving customers is spent listening to the rumor mill about what is coming next.

- **Lack of communication.** You must keep your employees in the loop. One of the biggest mistakes managers make with their customer service employees is not keeping employees informed and up to date on key changes and decisions within the company. Managers must share what they know, including decisions-in-progress and what is still undecided. This will build more loyalty and trust with their employees, which translates into a climate of motivation instead of demotivation.

A staffing firm found they had very low employee morale. The owner instituted monthly conference calls with the entire company to discuss management decisions point-by-point and set up an e-mail address to collect employee ideas. He then responded to each one personally. His employees are performing and serving the customers better.

One suggestion: carry an employee idea notebook and capture suggestions, complaints and questions from employees. Then follow up. Employees will respond by becoming more motivated.

- **Punishing people for good performance.** When someone goes the extra mile and does a good job handling a tough task or problem while her peers are goofing off or just doing enough to get by, what happens? Do you give her even more work? You will soon have a demotivated employee. She will soon learn not to do a good job because the result will be even more work.

A materials handling department in a plant had this problem. A few people seemed to do all the work in serving customers. They soon learned that those who did good work got assigned more. Soon, everyone was doing the least they could to get by and still not get fired. The manager never did figure it out.

- **Allowing poor performance to continue.** When you know someone is not doing their job, yet you allow it to continue, you create a big demotivator.

A customer service representative in a small office was just doing enough to stay employed. She spent a lot of time on personal phone calls and justified it by saying that she didn't "schmooze" and waste time like other employees. Five minutes before quitting time, she had her desk cleared off and refused to take any other customer calls for fear it would interfere with quitting time. Her manager did nothing about it. This caused the other employees to emulate her behavior, thinking, "If she can do it, so can we." Others may think, "That's not fair," another powerful demotivator.

- **Compensation systems that do not reward good behavior.** A hospital has an appraisal system with only three choices:

The employee is:

- Performing below standards

- Meeting or exceeding standards

- Walking on water

The problem is with the "meeting or exceeding standards." Those two behaviors need to be rewarded in different ways, not with the same percentage increase for each. The person who is exceeding the performance standards will become demotivated when he sees that the person who is just meeting the standards gets the same increase he does. He will figure, "Why bother," and go back to doing just an acceptable job.

In order to create a climate of motivation for your employees to consistently deliver superior service, you must incorporate many things. Just one action won't work. It must be a combination of both internal and external motivators, delivered often and sincerely.

Managers must have a style of interacting with people in ways that enhance self-esteem. They must listen carefully and respectfully to their employees. They must use goal-setting that challenges people supportively, providing them with clear, attainable steps to improved performance. And they must, from the time a new employee is hired to when they leave, make them feel special and an important member of the team.

Make the Workplace "Fun."

The Society for Human Resource Management (SHRM) surveyed 574 randomly selected members in a "Fun Work Environment Survey." The results of the survey showed that the number of its members who believe fun "...is very important in today's workplace is nearly double the number that was reporting that it was very important five years ago."

Some benefits of a "fun" atmosphere were:

- Increased employee enthusiasm (50% of respondents)

- Increased communication among employees and employee satisfaction (93%)

- Greater employee commitment to the organization (88%)

- Increased customer satisfaction (86%)

- Decreased employee anxiety and stress (84%)

- Fewer complaints of boredom (82%)

- Lower turnover (79%)

- Less absenteeism (72%)

- Fewer interpersonal conflicts (72%)

The Louisiana Department of Transportation and Development Federal Credit Union, headed by Cary Anderson, CEO, awarded an employee a big "cheese head" for the outstanding job done on a credit card conversion. The cheese head hat is passed around to employees who have successfully implemented and navigated a change that is helpful to their members. The cheese idea is based on the book, *Who Moved My Cheese?* by Spencer Johnson, MD.

When the credit union was having a great year, way ahead on its goals, Anderson sent everyone a congratulatory e-mail and personally visited each employee and presented them with a Wal-Mart gift card.

Use some of the ideas in this chapter to make your organization a fun and motivating place to work. Chapter Twelve also discusses some ideas on how to put fun into your workplace.

HOW GOOD ARE YOU AT MOTIVATION QUIZ

Please check the methods you are currently using to create a climate of motivation in your organization.

_____ External, tangible rewards—money, gifts, trips, meals, special parking spaces, etc.

_____ Frequent verbal praise

_____ Fun activities

_____ Written praise, thank you notes, letters

_____ Special achievement awards

_____ Formal awards like multi-level awards programs, personal growth opportunities, etc.

_____ "If you...then..." awards

_____ Conditional awards

_____ Surprise awards

Scoring

9-8 checks: Congratulations! You probably have a very motivated workforce. Keep up the good work.

7-5 checks: You're doing a pretty good job, but you need to implement some other motivational tools in order to have your employees continually motivated to offer excellent service.

Less than 5 checks: You need to do some serious work on your motivational tools. Choose two items above that you are not currently using and add them to your motivational plan.

Customer Service: How to Do It Right!

CHAPTER ELEVEN

Coaching for Performance Improvement

Your newly hired customer service representative is not handling your customers well. Several of them have complained that he is short and rude with them and he seems to have a bad attitude. You have observed him serving your customers and he doesn't smile, give good eye contact or know everything he should about the product or service. Yet he went through the customer service training and should be behaving differently. So what's the problem?

Surprise! People don't always do what you tell them to do. You can orient, train, praise and reward them, yet they still don't treat customers the way you would like them to. To decrease the number of incidents where people say employees are rude, discourteous and delivering poor customer service, you must become actively involved in coaching your employees.

Shaping the behavior of your employees is not an easy thing to do. It's hard enough to change ourselves, much less try to change someone else. One of the most important tools in developing employees who consistently deliver exceptional service is coaching them on a regular basis.

Once you have explained and taught the behavior you expect, you must measure it and work with the employee who does not live not up to your standards. You must remain respectful yet firm in order to achieve the best results. There must be consequences for not exhibiting good customer service behaviors.

Try to avoid blaming all poor customer service behavior on an employee's "bad attitude." (That is so vague and general you will never get the behavior change you want.) If you just dismiss poor service behavior as an "attitude problem," you will never be able to get the best from that employee.

You must determine the exact behaviors the employee exhibits that make you and your customers feel she has a bad attitude. Is she often late to work? Does she not return the customers' phone calls in a timely manner or take the time to listen to all the customers have to say? Does she have what you perceive to be a negative expression on her face all the time? Is her tone of voice sharp, and does she hurry the callers through the service process? If you can't come up with specifics, you will never be able to effectively coach the employee to deliver exceptional customer service.

Use the ratings from the Customer Service Ratings Worksheet in Chapter Nine to determine areas of performance gaps and to see where they might need some coaching. Tailor the evaluation to the different jobs of your employees.

After you have observed and assessed any gaps in performance, you must decide whether it is:

1. **A knowledge problem.** They don't know how to do it—somehow the training didn't stick, or they are not getting enough coaching to help them learn the job. Maybe they didn't take the time to learn the products they are selling, for instance, or maybe they don't know how to do something. For example, a salesperson in an electronics store who doesn't know the different features and benefits of the different kinds of printers cannot possibly deliver exceptional service.

2. **A skills problem.** They physically or mentally can't do the job, or else someone or something keeps them from doing it. A lack of resources or too little time are possible impediments.

3. **An attitude problem.** They could do the job well if their life depended on it, but for some reason they are not doing it. They could be burned out, unhappy with their manager or job or maybe previous good work went unrecognized.

If it is a knowledge problem, send them back through training to help them learn what they need to perform the job well. If it is a skills problem, they may respond to more training; however, they may just be in the wrong job. But if it is an "attitude problem," you must coach the employee to help them improve their behavior.

You must clearly and quickly communicate job expectations to the poorly performing employee. Don't make the mistake of calling your employees together and chastising them all, thinking that the poorly performing employee will get the message. Usually they don't. They think you are talking about someone else. You must give the problem employee individual coaching in order to improve his performance.

Before you begin the coaching process to change unsatisfactory on-the-job behavior, decide three things:

1. Decide what minimum action is acceptable as the outcome of the discussion.

Is it that the employee report for work on time consistently? Or that each customer be greeted with a smile as they walk in the door?

2. Do alternatives exist that may improve the behavior?

If they are late for work, for instance, can you adjust their hours somewhat so that they can better meet the schedule?

3. What is the timetable for performance improvement?

Must the behavior change start in one week? Immediately? Establish deadlines and give the employee progress reports.

Next, meet with the employee in a private spot and start the coaching session with some opening statements like:

"I want to tell you some things that are getting in the way of your success here."

"I have noticed some errors that are not a sample of your usual good work. Tell me what happened."

"Let me tell you why we are here. I am concerned about…"

"I need to make you aware of a situation that has come to my attention."

When coaching employees toward better customer service behaviors, use the DESC technique:

- Describe

- Express

- Specify

- Consequences/collaborate

Describe the behavior in specific terms. Concentrate on the person's performance, not personality. Don't say, "You have a negative attitude" or "You are not a team player."

Instead, you will need to talk about the actual behaviors you see that cause you and your customers to feel the employee is not delivering exceptional service. Be specific about what the employee has done over what length of time and how that compares to the expected behavior.

A good way to help you make sure you focus on the performance and not the personality is to start your coaching with the statement, "When you...".

"When you came in late for your shift...".

"When you do not greet our customers with a smile...".

"When you do not stop what you are doing to attend to the customer...".

Express the problems it causes for you, the business and your customers.

"When you come in late for your shift, it causes us to be understaffed and not able to deliver exceptional customer service."

"When you do not greet our customers with a smile it causes our customers to receive a poor impression of the business."

"When you do not stop what you are doing to attend to the customers, it causes them to feel they are not important."

Now you have two choices in how you coach your employee. You should choose which makes the most sense in the individual situation. You can either specify exactly what behavior you expect from the employee and then talk about either positive or negative consequences, or you can use the collaboration method. The collaboration method engages the employee in a discussion about what they would suggest for a solution to the problem.

Specify exactly what behavior change you expect and state the consequences if the behavior is not changed. Sometimes you can even think of a positive consequence. Express confidence in the employee's ability to correct the behavior and praise the employee at the first sign of improvement. Use an "if...then" statement.

"When you arrive late for your shift, it causes us to be understaffed and to be unable to deliver exceptional service. So in the future, I want you to be on time. If you don't, I will need to write you up and begin the disciplinary process."

"When you do not greet our customers with a smile, it causes them to receive a poor impression of the business. In the future, I would like you to greet each customer with a smile, both in person and on the telephone. I think you will find that smiling will put your customers in a good mood and make them easier for you to deal with."

"When you do not stop what you are doing to attend to the customers, it causes them to feel they are not important, and it makes them not want to do future business with us. I want you to immediately stop what you are doing and welcome each customer as they come up to the service desk. I know you probably haven't realized you were doing this and can easily correct it."

Collaborate with the employee on how to improve the behavior.

If the situation doesn't call for specifying and stating consequences, you can use the collaboration approach.

"When you arrive late for your shift, it causes us to be understaffed and unable to deliver exceptional service. Tell me why you are having trouble getting in on time and what you think you can do about it."

"When you do not greet our customers with a smile, it causes them to receive a poor impression of the business. Is there some reason you are unable to do this?"

"When you do not stop what you are doing to attend to the customers, it causes them to feel they are not important, and it makes them not want to do future business with us. Is there something in our systems and procedures that is preventing you from doing this?"

Remember to demonstrate assertive body language as you use the DESC techniques. Maintain direct eye contact and an erect, alert body posture while speaking clearly with a high-energy authority level.

There are four possibilities for performance improvement:

1. Increased use of the behaviors

2. Decreased incidences of the behaviors

3. Additional behaviors

4. Improved behaviors

that every employee can change and will change when change
rthwhile to them. You must make this "want to" factor take root if
ve your employees exhibit the desired behavior even when you are

at your employees want to do the work. When you expect that
ill offer exceptional service, you will behave toward them in a way
that come true. When you take a negative attitude toward your
assuming that they don't want to perform well, they will tend to
n, to that expectation. If you really want an employee to do well,
ve that he will do the work at a high level.

"If you treat an individual as he is he will stay that way, but if you
e were what he could be, he will become what he could be."

sually become interested in changing their behavior when they
stand how their current behavior is hurting them or how they
enefit from behaving differently. So as you are coaching, you must
benefits of changing and ask for a performance change. If you
sually just get worse.

nt out how particular behaviors will produce better results for
ore likely to change their behaviors. Try to find out some of the
yee values and tie the benefits to that. Are they concerned
, for instance? Or is recognition a turn-on for them? Build those
coaching session.

to inadvertently reward the poor behavior by giving the
rly scheduled raise, for instance, when they are still exhibiting
rvice behaviors.

tems

mployee's performance, both behaviors that need improve-
y are already doing right, is also important. Consider using an
em. This will give you specific behaviors that you can reward
need improvement.

Using the DESC technique, help the employee to determine how they will improve their customer service behaviors through the use of one or several of these choices. Then have the employee make a written action plan and a commitment to the behavior change. Ask, "What questions do you have," to encourage them to ask questions, instead of, "Do you have any questions," to make sure that you have made yourself clear.

Monitor the employee's progress and set specific times when you and the employee will discuss their progress. You must get an employee to recognize and agree that she needs to improve and change, or the coaching will fail. Without agreement, there is little likelihood that there will be any improvement or that it will be a permanent change.

Don't assume that the employee sees the situation or the solution the same way you do. Remember that the employee is working within his comfort zone and doing what comes naturally. He likes what he is doing. It will be uncomfortable for him to change his behavior, so unless you can convince the employee that it is in his best interest to change, he will be resistant to the change.

Dealing with Resistance

It would be wonderful if the above information worked all the time, but unfortunately it doesn't. You will sometimes run into resistance from the employee you are trying to coach.

Watch for these signs of resistance:

- Emotion. It can be an angry retort or crying.

- "But you are my friend. How can you do this to me?"

- Changing the subject.

- Refusing to believe the information.

- Excuses.

- Defiant acceptance.

When you run into situations like these, try some of these tactics.

1. **Postpone the discussion.** "Ashley, I can see that I need to let you have a little time to think about this. Why don't we schedule another meeting tomorrow morning so we can discuss this further?"

2. **Monitor.** Keep a closer-than-usual watch on the employee's behavior and make frequent reminders about the behavior change you expect.

3. **Encourage.** Suspend any criticism for a while and look for every opportunity to praise the employee and maintain a positive focus.

Do's and Don'ts of Coaching

Do's:

- Help them develop a plan to acquire the skills needed to be successful with customers.

- Remember: Be clear about what the performance deficiency is. Don't say, "You have a bad attitude." Figure out the specific behaviors that are making you feel the employee has an attitude problem.

- Do all of your homework and be sure of your facts. Dig deeply to get as much information as you can and try to observe the behavior yourself. Know all the details of the performance gap.

- Talk with the employee as soon as possible. Don't put it off. It will just make matters worse.

- Be prepared with specific examples of the behaviors you have observed that are customer unfriendly.

- Listen carefully to the employee's side of the story.

- Get the employee involved in devising the solution. Work with the employee to come up with a specific action plan or change of behaviors that will occur.

- Make sure the employee commits to the behavior change you want.

- Choose a good time and a private place.

- Maintain a sincere, helpful attitude.

- Be straightforward, calm and businessli[ke] your feelings and stay calm.

- Plan and even rehearse your words ahe[ad]

- Keep accurate records of coaching inc[idents]

Don't:

- Beat around the bush. Come to the p[oint] the breeze.

- Jump to conclusions based on your [own]

- Assume the employee can't handle [not] improving.

- Accuse. Don't do something that [is] calling.

- Bring only negative messages all th[e]

- Get defensive yourself when emp[loyee]

- Smile too much. It will send the [wrong]

- Keep repeating the feedback yo[u] are given, you've done it.

- Exaggerate. Don't say, "You're al[ways]... ing recipient to argue with the [real] issue.

- Refer to anonymous people. [It looks like] you are not being responsive

- Fail to receive a commitmen[t and] consequences for failing to [comply]

Rememb[er] becomes wo[rse] you aim to ha[ve] not there.

Assume th[at] your people w[ill] that will make [something of] employees by [something] live up, or dow[n] you must belie[ve]

Goethe said treat him as if [he is]

Employees u[nderstand] come to under[stand] could possibly b[e] show them the ignore it, it will [continue]

When you po[sition] them, they are m[ore likely to do] things the empl[oyee] about job securit[y] rewards into the

Be careful not [to give] employee a regula[r diet of] poor customer se[rvice]

Tracking Sys[tem]

Tracking your e[mploy]ment and things the incident report sys[tem] or coach when the[y]

Using the DESC technique, help the employee to determine how they will improve their customer service behaviors through the use of one or several of these choices. Then have the employee make a written action plan and a commitment to the behavior change. Ask, "What questions do you have," to encourage them to ask questions, instead of, "Do you have any questions," to make sure that you have made yourself clear.

Monitor the employee's progress and set specific times when you and the employee will discuss their progress. You must get an employee to recognize and agree that she needs to improve and change, or the coaching will fail. Without agreement, there is little likelihood that there will be any improvement or that it will be a permanent change.

Don't assume that the employee sees the situation or the solution the same way you do. Remember that the employee is working within his comfort zone and doing what comes naturally. He likes what he is doing. It will be uncomfortable for him to change his behavior, so unless you can convince the employee that it is in his best interest to change, he will be resistant to the change.

Dealing with Resistance

It would be wonderful if the above information worked all the time, but unfortunately it doesn't. You will sometimes run into resistance from the employee you are trying to coach.

Watch for these signs of resistance:

- Emotion. It can be an angry retort or crying.

- "But you are my friend. How can you do this to me?"

- Changing the subject.

- Refusing to believe the information.

- Excuses.

- Defiant acceptance.

When you run into situations like these, try some of these tactics.

1. **Postpone the discussion.** "Ashley, I can see that I need to let you have a little time to think about this. Why don't we schedule another meeting tomorrow morning so we can discuss this further?"

2. **Monitor.** Keep a closer-than-usual watch on the employee's behavior and make frequent reminders about the behavior change you expect.

3. **Encourage.** Suspend any criticism for a while and look for every opportunity to praise the employee and maintain a positive focus.

Do's and Don'ts of Coaching

Do's:

- Help them develop a plan to acquire the skills needed to be successful with customers.

- Remember: Be clear about what the performance deficiency is. Don't say, "You have a bad attitude." Figure out the specific behaviors that are making you feel the employee has an attitude problem.

- Do all of your homework and be sure of your facts. Dig deeply to get as much information as you can and try to observe the behavior yourself. Know all the details of the performance gap.

- Talk with the employee as soon as possible. Don't put it off. It will just make matters worse.

- Be prepared with specific examples of the behaviors you have observed that are customer unfriendly.

- Listen carefully to the employee's side of the story.

- Get the employee involved in devising the solution. Work with the employee to come up with a specific action plan or change of behaviors that will occur.

- Make sure the employee commits to the behavior change you want.

- Choose a good time and a private place.

- Maintain a sincere, helpful attitude.

- Be straightforward, calm and businesslike. Don't get emotional. Control your feelings and stay calm.

- Plan and even rehearse your words ahead of time.

- Keep accurate records of coaching incidents.

Don't:

- Beat around the bush. Come to the point quickly. Don't start with shooting the breeze.

- Jump to conclusions based on your own biases.

- Assume the employee can't handle the feedback or is not interested in improving.

- Accuse. Don't do something that will cause more problems, like name calling.

- Bring only negative messages all the time.

- Get defensive yourself when employees "push back" during coaching.

- Smile too much. It will send the wrong message.

- Keep repeating the feedback you are giving. Once the development ideas are given, you've done it.

- Exaggerate. Don't say, "You're always late for deadlines." It invites the coaching recipient to argue with the exaggeration rather than respond to the real issue.

- Refer to anonymous people. Avoid statements such as, "Everybody feels you are not being responsive to our customers."

- Fail to receive a commitment on performance improvement or to discuss consequences for failing to do so.

Remember that every employee can change and will change when change becomes worthwhile to them. You must make this "want to" factor take root if you aim to have your employees exhibit the desired behavior even when you are not there.

Assume that your employees want to do the work. When you expect that your people will offer exceptional service, you will behave toward them in a way that will make that come true. When you take a negative attitude toward your employees by assuming that they don't want to perform well, they will tend to live up, or down, to that expectation. If you really want an employee to do well, you must believe that he will do the work at a high level.

Goethe said: "If you treat an individual as he is he will stay that way, but if you treat him as if he were what he could be, he will become what he could be."

Employees usually become interested in changing their behavior when they come to understand how their current behavior is hurting them or how they could possibly benefit from behaving differently. So as you are coaching, you must show them the benefits of changing and ask for a performance change. If you ignore it, it will usually just get worse.

When you point out how particular behaviors will produce better results for them, they are more likely to change their behaviors. Try to find out some of the things the employee values and tie the benefits to that. Are they concerned about job security, for instance? Or is recognition a turn-on for them? Build those rewards into the coaching session.

Be careful not to inadvertently reward the poor behavior by giving the employee a regularly scheduled raise, for instance, when they are still exhibiting poor customer service behaviors.

Tracking Systems

Tracking your employee's performance, both behaviors that need improvement and things they are already doing right, is also important. Consider using an incident report system. This will give you specific behaviors that you can reward or coach when they need improvement.

When your employees do something over and beyond their job responsibilities, enter it on their incident report. When they do not handle a customer well, don't meet their deadlines or in some way give poor service, write that down too. This will help create a top-of-the-mind awareness of how everything they do is important in delivering exceptional customer service.

Employees may see their sheet at any time, and it serves as a constant reinforcer to help them think about every action they take with customers. You will soon find your employees asking you to be sure to record positive actions on their incident report. And when you make an entry of poor performance, employees will strive to do something good to overcome that statement.

Make sure that you check the reports at least once a month to ensure that information is accumulated on each employee every month. This will force you to notice what is happening, especially the good things. Coaching is about noticing the good things and reinforcing those as well as the behaviors that need improvement.

Remember that coaching is something you do to improve behavior but not at the cost of the employee's self-esteem. You want to help without humiliating. Try to make the employee realize that when you criticize his performance, it is to help him gain greater skills that will help him in the future, both with his present and future jobs.

If you bend the rules or fail to coach one low-performing employee, it will impact the rest of your staff and produce low levels of morale and, therefore, performance. "If he can come in late, why can't I" is the way the thinking goes. That's why coaching, along with positive reinforcement mentioned in the previous chapter, must be an important part of your customer service program. Based on what you have read so far and your own experience, complete the following coaching plan.

Coaching Action Plan

1. My most effective coaching skills are:

2. My coaching skills need improvement in these areas:

3. I will do the following to improve my coaching skills:

4. Barriers that I will face in improving my coaching skills:

5. Ways that I will overcome these barriers:

CHAPTER TWELVE

Retention of Your Employees—It's Not Always about the Paycheck

Once you have hired and trained your employees, then you must retain them. After all, how can you possibly deliver superior service if your employees are going out the back door as fast as you can bring them in the front? Keeping your turnover rate low is a major key to developing and delivering superior customer service.

Take this quick retention test. You know you have a workplace where employees will stay with you longer if they:

1. Work hard to improve themselves, thus increasing their value to you and themselves.

2. Recruit their friends to also come work at your company.

3. Make personal sacrifices to ensure the success of your organization.

4. Feel that their workplace is one of the best around.

Retention used to be much easier, right? Pay them enough, give them good benefits, and have a picnic or some other employee event once a year. Even your part-time or temporary help seemed to stay longer in previous years. Now your employees want more. And in order to deliver that "more," you must develop an entire culture of retention that answers the needs of three or even four generations in the workplace.

Many of the issues we talked about in the previous chapters on motivation and coaching will contribute to a good retention rate and the culture that sustains it. However, there are other factors that must be in place in order to establish a culture of retention. There is no one "magic bullet" that you can institute that will increase your retention rate. Rather, it is a combination of things in your culture that all add up to building an organization where people love to come to work. It will enable you to become an employer of choice.

Retaining employees is all about creating a "Total Employment Experience." Get over the idea that retention is found in employee paychecks. Outstanding benefits and pay alone will not help you retain your employees. In fact, 55 percent of workers say they will "jump ship" for a pay increase of twenty percent or less. More than 23 percent would leave for an increase of 10 percent or less.

Minimum wage workers are often desperate for a pay increase. They may leave you for someone else offering 25 cents an hour more. A waitress at a national restaurant chain felt that her manager was "more of a friend" but still left to work at another restaurant because of 50 cents more an hour.

So your wages must be in the ballpark to be competitive, but you must also consider other elements. Even in traditionally high turnover industries like hospitality, help desks, fast-food restaurants and retail stores, your turnover rate can be lowered if you work to establish a culture for retention. And when your turnover rate is low, your customer service is better.

According to a study by the Hays Group, the following are top reasons for people staying in their jobs. Ninety percent of respondents listed at least one of the first three items among the top three or four reasons they stayed.

1. Career growth, learning and development.

2. Exciting work and challenge.

3. Meaningful work, making a difference and a contribution.

4. Great people.

5. Being part of a team.

6. Good boss.

7. Recognition for work well done.

8. Fun on the job.

9. Autonomy—sense of control over my work.

10. Flexibility—for example, in work hours and dress code.

11. Fair pay and benefits.

12. Inspiring leadership.

13. Pride in the organization, its mission and quality of product.

14. Great work environment.

15. Location.

16. Job security.

17. Family-friendly.

18. Cutting-edge technology.

A Gallup Poll found that 50 percent of work-life satisfaction is determined by the relationship a worker has with his boss, and that the length of an employee's stay at an organization is largely determined by his relationship with his supervisor. Sharon Jordan Evans, in the book, *Love 'Em or Lose 'Em* says, People don't quit jobs, they quit bosses."

The Cost of Turnover

Have you ever figured how much money you are losing because of lack of employee retention? One company calculated the cost of hiring one new employee for their help desk to be $3000—$2500 for recruiting and $500 to process the paperwork. But this was only the tip of the cost iceberg. Until the new hire got up to speed, she would not be able to work as productively or answer customers' questions as effectively. Customer service suffered while the new employee learned her job. How much was that worth?

A major communications company learned that a new hire can only accomplish 60 percent as much in the first three months as an experienced worker. And even a 5 percent drop in efficiency can cut revenue by a significant amount.

Then there are the intangibles, like loss of morale, increased employee stress for those still in the department and a negative reputation. ("Oh yeah, I hear that company is a regular revolving door.")

Figures differ, but replacing an employee costs roughly one and one-half times a year's pay. Advertising costs, recruitment dollars, interviewing time, training time, the loss of productivity while the positions are vacant and the expense of temporary help all become subtractions from the bottom line.

Try calculating your current cost of turnover:

Your cost of acquiring that employee in the
first place, including salary, benefits and
agency fees, if you used one.   _____

Cost of orientation and training time.   _____

Working time lost until full employee
productivity is achieved.   _____

Total   _____

That's how much the turnover of one employee will cost you.

For example:

Cost of acquisition of employee:

Advertising:	$3000
Time spent interviewing	3000
Cost of orientation and training time	6000
Working time lost until full employee productivity	8000
	————
Total:	$20,000

Research shows that the average employee entering the workforce of today will have five careers or jobs throughout their working career. So where does this leave you when people are constantly shifting from job to job? In an environment where it is hard to run a business and to consistently deliver exceptional service.

Here are the elements that go into creating a culture of retention.

The 5 Rs of Retention

1. Responsibility, challenge and career paths

2. Rules, goals and expectations

3. Respect

4. Rewards, recognition and benefits

5. Revelry

Responsibility, challenge and career paths

Responsibility, challenge and empowerment

If your employees feel they have no say in how they do their jobs and no sense of responsibility for the results, you will lose them. Empowerment plays a big part in making an employee feel they wield some power in determining the day to day parts of their job.

Empowerment is defined in many ways. Mainly it is the feeling that the employee has a sense of choice about how he does the job. It is a feeling that he has the freedom to make decisions and even mistakes. To feel empowered is to feel a sense of control, a sense that you have the power to affect the work and the organization with your efforts.

Darryl Hartley-Leonard, when he was President of Hyatt Hotels Corporation, said, "Empowerment is the recognition that employees are not as dumb as employers thought they were."

Booker T. Washington put it this way: "Few things help an individual more than to place responsibility on him, and let him know that you trust him."

So if a customer has a problem, do your employees have to run to a manager to deal with it? Or do they have some parameters within which they can solve the situation for the customer? The more control they have within their job, the happier they will be and the more likely to stay with you.

One manager's employees were pressuring her to develop a policy on alternative work schedules (AWS). She responded by giving them full responsibility for designing a form she could use to explore the feasibility of AWS requests. Then she gave full credit to the involved employees at a department meeting where she asked for reactions to the form. "Can this be our policy," she wanted to know. In delegating authority with responsibility, this manager generated a new policy that became the prototype for her employer.

Set "ranges" of appropriate decision-making. Whenever possible, set boundaries rather than establishing strict rules and procedures. For instance, if a customer is unhappy with his meal, the server can be empowered to give them a free dessert or take a certain percentage off the bill, depending on the severity of the mistake. Or a customer service representative can be empowered to refund an unhappy customer the late charge on an overdue bill, if the customer claims they never received the bill.

Watch for an instance in which someone takes a risk in order to make a customer happy and it doesn't work. Celebrate the failure and coach them in a non-threatening way on how to make it better the next time. Take the time to ask your employees what could be done differently when they don't perform to your expectations, rather than just taking away any decision-making powers.

If you find that your employees are making the wrong decisions, it will usually be for three reasons:

1. Not enough training.

2. Not enough information.

3. Not enough skill. You have the wrong person for the job.

Personal empowerment assumes that each employee has the ability to do the job and that they will do it as well as they know how. Most organizations that have successfully empowered their employees have given them training in problem-solving and decision-making.

Ask frequently, "What makes your job difficult to do?" Get your employees to make suggestions as to what barriers stand in the way of them doing a great job. It is a big demotivator when company policies and procedures or lack of supplies make the employee's job difficult to do.

Career Paths or Room to Grow

A Generation Xer, Ashley, has a very well-paying job in San Francisco as the customer service manager of a large department. She has great benefits and other perks. But she feels that she has already learned everything she can in this particular position and there is little room for advancement.

She plans to quit her job and move to New York City, with no immediate prospects for a job there. She wants a job with new challenges and learning opportunities. Ashley is like many Generation Xers. Learning and challenges are a large part of what keeps her on the job.

When employees decide to change jobs, they typically do it after coming to the conclusion that they have no opportunity for growth in their present position. Generation X and Y employees are particularly susceptible to this. Russell J. Campanello, Chief People Officer at Nerve Wire Inc., when interviewed in *Fast Company Magazine*, relates that the number-one reason people leave their jobs is to pursue personal development—the chance to learn something new.

But that doesn't apply to all age ranges. As your employees get closer to retirement, retirement benefits and job security become more important. On the other hand, minimum-wage earners of any age will still be more focused on money.

Forty-one percent of Human Relations and other executives polled in a US survey ranked "limited advancement potential" as the number-one factor in staff turnover. They maintained that companies' failure to promote from within or clearly communicate advancement opportunities caused a worker migration to the companies that do.

Randalls Supermarkets found that offering their employees a career ladder is one of the retention ideas that works for them. A lot of their current managers started as checkers and are now store directors or managers. Even their president started out checking groceries.

Employees can "self nominate" themselves for the company's management training program, and the current managers are always on the lookout for good candidates. They also have a mentor program that is effective in their retention strategy. The supermarket's associates are selected for the mentor program or they can ask to be mentored.

Of course, the chain also offers fair wages in line with the current market, good benefits and excellent working conditions. That is a given. If you don't start with those, you will never be able to retain your employees, no matter what else you do.

But what if there is no room for advancement? Here are some ideas:

- Collapse salary levels and job grades so that position descriptions overlap. This allows employees to apply for more jobs within grade and also gives managers more people to choose from.

- Consider short-term transfers across departments to introduce employees to new skills and to uncover talents you didn't know your employees had.

- Make it easier to change jobs within the company and to make lateral moves.

- Add job titles and levels. For instance, an entry-level position could be simply called "Customer Service Consultant." Then add a II or III to the title as they gain in experience and time with the company. Then you could have a "Senior Customer Service Consultant" level with additional numbers.

One fast-food restaurant has different colors for uniforms as employees move up in length of employment. It has become a matter of pride among employees to move up a color. The final color is given after an employee's third year.

Training, especially cross-training of employees, is an effective retention and career development tool. Eric Rabinowitz, President of HIS Helpdesk Service, as quoted in *Customer Support Management Magazine*, says, "Training plays a powerful role in retention." By implementing a new training program, they increased the average length of employment for analysts from five to 12 months.

The Gallup Organization research found that 80 percent of employees are more likely to stay with a company if they receive regular training. Four in 10 workers say training is a very important factor in determining whether they will stay with a company. Another 4 in 10 rate it as "important."

Cross-training, teaching an employee more than one job, is an especially effective way to keep your employees growing and feeling they are learning skills that will help them move up the career ladder. It also makes your organization better able to deliver exceptional customer service. When employees know each other's jobs, they can keep from having to pass the customer around until the person who knows the answer to that particular question shows up.

A recently cross-trained employee at an HMO was overheard talking excitedly to a coworker about being able to adjust claims instead of just passing them up the ladder to someone else. She felt much more in control, and she was learning new skills.

Remember that training is not always sitting in a classroom. It is the constant feedback and coaching from managers that is sometimes the most powerful form of training. Regular, constructive performance reviews are also an important part of training.

A young employee, talking to a co-worker, said, "Experience without direction and feedback is wasted time. Only work for people from whom you can learn." That is why coaching, as discussed in the previous chapter, is such an important part of developing employees who can consistently deliver excellent service.

An Italian restaurant, which has been in business over 10 years and has an unusually low turnover rate, always asks their employees if they want to be trained for a new position when they have maxed out in the salary range at their current position.

Steve Lauer and B. Jack Gebhardt, writing in *Now Hiring! Finding and Keeping Good Help For Your Entry-Wage Jobs*, say, "Those jobs that continue to provide new experiences, new heights to climb, new arenas to master, are those jobs that will keep people around."

Rules, Goals and Expectations

But you can't empower every employee. Not everyone likes, or is capable of, being empowered. People are comfortable with different levels of rules and regulations. A key to managing and retaining your employees is to figure whether an employee needs lots of freedom to "do their own thing" or likes the stability of being told exactly what to do. Younger workers in their first or second job usually need more rules and parameters. Some employees feel more comfortable if they have some strict guidelines—they need boundaries.

Set specific expectations and goals for your employees and make them clear from the first hiring interview and throughout the first month on the job. If employees leave because the job differed from their expectations, it means the manager has not made clear what is expected of the workers.

A residential maid service tells their employees, "This is what we will give you and this is what you give us in return." Workers earn an attendance bonus every pay period if they have arrived at work every day on time and in uniform. That gives them an easily-understood expectation.

Managers at a maintenance supply company make the rules very clear for their truck drivers, and use bonuses for length of time with the company and for successfully staying within certain safety and other parameters.

The more you tell employees about the behaviors you expect, the more motivated and interested in their jobs they become. This goes back to the service goals or targets discussed in Chapter Four.

Setting Goals and Challenges

The communication of your direction or vision of the company and the employees' opportunities to participate in its success or failure is important in retention. So keep your mission/vision statement or service goals in front of your people at all times. Talk about it often, and help the employee see how his actions contribute to that mission.

Share the challenges your organization or team is facing and help people develop personal connections to the organization's success. When people can see the difference their work makes to the total organization, they will feel respected and invested and thus stay in the job longer.

People are naturally competitive. They will try to top whatever goals are set for them, whether or not they get more money in their paycheck. So create measurement and feedback systems that are motivating and relevant for the individual or team. If your employees have no way of knowing how much they are contributing to the success of the company, they will quickly look elsewhere for a place where they do make a difference.

Involve each employee in setting clear standards for productivity, as well as work quality and timeliness. Then make everyone responsible for meeting these standards. When the standards and expectations are not met, ask the employees what to do about it—don't dictate.

Respect

According to a study by Baxter Healthcare, the most basic work-life need of employees is respect from their employer. People in today's world are starving for respect and want to be considered as human beings in their places of work.

Respect is shown in so many ways. Does your company have reserved parking spaces for the managers, but none for the front-line employees—the ones who represent your company to the customers? That is a subtle way of saying "You are not as important as us." Is that something that will help in retaining your employees?

The best forms of respect are listening to and acknowledging your employees. Encourage employees to let you know what is on their minds. Make time for it. You don't have to approve, endorse or even react. Just listen.

Make Them Feel They Are an Important Part of the Team.

Respect your employees by letting them feel they are an integral part of the company, no matter what their position in the hierarchy. Communicate information about the company on a regular basis. Be honest. Share new plans and the reasons for them. Be consistent in the handling of employees, and do not show favoritism.

Managers at a major supermarket chain show they respect all their workers. They emphasize diversity by publishing the company newsletter in both Spanish and English. They feel this says to the employees, "We care about you."

Be sure that what you say and do are congruent. Don't signal right and then turn left. A CEO of a small benefits company preached that being on time to work was of utmost importance, yet he was always late. When employees are held to different standards than others, they perceive that a basic unfairness exists and will begin looking around for another job.

An employee of a small retail store chain attended a meeting where the president asked for questions from the floor at the end of her presentation. After a few minutes' hesitation, one brave employee raised his hand and asked a question. The president then proceeded to give the impression that she thought that was the stupidest question ever asked. There were no more questions asked at that or any future meetings. Is it any wonder that the retail chain has major turnover problems?

Listen to Your Employees' Ideas and Suggestions.

A lack of respect diminishes employees' willingness to participate. A group of hospital housekeepers recently got a new boss after a long-time supervisor retired. For the first time in 15 years, they began to offer suggestions for work improvements. When asked why, the workers said their new boss treated them with respect, invited them to share in decision-making and always said, "Hello," when she saw them—something the previous boss had never done.

So keep asking, "How can we do things differently for you and for the company?" Develop a system where you can capture employees' ideas on how to improve service and other ideas that will help the company be more profitable. Even if the ideas are something that will make the employees' jobs easier or more comfortable to do, it will benefit the company in the long run.

A hotel manager initiated an employee suggestion program. But in the beginning, all they got were ideas on how to make the employees' jobs easier or provide them with small perks like picnic tables outside so they could eat lunch under the trees. The manager was able to make many of those things happen. But then the ideas started pouring in about how to cut costs and make the hotel more profitable. The employees were convinced that their managers did indeed respect their opinions and cared about them.

Survey your employees on a regular basis. Find out where the problems are before they walk out the door. It can be a simple suggestion box or a more elaborate paper survey. Just do something to get your employees' ideas and suggestions to show that you respect them.

Give Them Help with Issues Outside of Work.

This is a factor that often comes into play with minimum-wage workers. Things like child care, transportation, immigration issues, language skills and everyday transactions can be problems to some of your employees. Until some of these needs are addressed, your employees won't be able to do their jobs effectively and will often leave. The more you can help them with personal issues, the more they will feel respected.

One major hotel chain set up a special "customer service" department for workers. One employee in the human relations department was available to help workers fill out the paperwork to get food stamps, arrange for child care, make loans and handle immigration matters.

The owner of a small restaurant often helps his employees with personal issues that interfere with them getting to work on a regular basis. In order to be kept aware of workers' needs, he routinely ate lunch with employees so he could learn who needed what assistance. A resort hotel manager hires buses to bring employees to the worksite because many cannot afford transportation.

Respect Your Employees' Quality of Life

Your employees want help balancing work and family obligations. Employees are working for a living, but if they can't take a day off, they will soon look elsewhere. Companies that are sensitive to the fact that employees have lives outside the office are better able to retain workers.

Workers talk to each other about their jobs and whether they leave time for a life. Word gets around concerning which companies are the best to work for. Younger employees are especially concerned with having time for play.

Look at how much overtime you are demanding. Do your employees have to choose between work and family life? Do you make them feel that taking off early to see their child in a play is wrong? Companies like this will have a more difficult time getting their good people to stay.

Give your employees some flexibility in how they work and when they work. A major department store touts their policy where employees can choose their own hours and days. It makes it harder to schedule, yes, but they have also upped their retention rate.

Putt Putt FunHouse, mentioned in previous chapters, is very flexible about their employees' schedules where school activities are concerned. The owner, Jim

Saxe, feels that kids who engage in extracurricular activities make better employees, so he makes it possible for them to trade days with other employees and to have enough flexibility to be able to continue in those activities while they work for him.

Ask your current employees about whether your policies leave them feeling out of balance and burned out. If the answer is "yes," ask for suggestions on how you can change those policies to be more balance-friendly. Design some flexibility into your work schedules and you will attract and retain the kind of candidates who will stay with you.

Rewards, Recognition and Benefits

Rewards and recognition have been covered in Chapter Thirteen, but benefits are also important in your overall retention plan. Today, employees are looking for good benefits as well as other factors.

In the restaurant business and other industries where benefits are traditionally few, offering even minimal healthcare benefits will increase your attraction and retention rates. Consider offering employees educational reimbursement, profit sharing or a company-matched 401(k) plan after they have been with you a certain length of time.

According to a survey by Aon Consulting, the most important benefits that will translate into retention are those benefits that offer a stake in the future success or failure of a company. So see if stock purchase/ownership plans, profit-sharing or cash bonus plans and defined benefit plans will fit into your organization.

Also important are well-designed, flexible work schedules, availability of counseling, benefit choice and preventative medical care programs. How effective you are in communicating the value of your benefits is also key in keeping your employees.

An employer of many truck drivers found their turnover rate dropped after they started communicating just how much their benefits were worth in dollars and cents. The drivers often didn't realize their value until they had left the company for what they thought were higher-paying jobs, only to find they were getting fewer benefits.

Customer Service: How to Do It Right!

Revelry

As mentioned in Chapter Ten, employees today want to have some fun in the workplace. This is especially true of Generation X and Y. If your employees enjoy coming to work most of the time, they will be happier, more productive and stay with you longer.

The intentional use of fun in your workplace is an important part of developing a culture of retention. Studies show that we need the healing powers of laughter and play during times of stress and pressure. Plus, sharing a laugh with someone is a great way to build the relationships that teams depend on. When people have laughed together, it is easier for them to overlook the differences that cause trouble and, therefore, cut down on productivity.

But, of course, not all humor and fun is appropriate for the workplace. You need to determine what will work in your organization. Learn from people who use humor well. Observe what seems to work. Who is able to create a fun atmosphere while still getting the job done?

Fun in the workplace does not create a victim. It must rely on lighthearted activities rather than elaborate jokes played on someone else. Who creates a little humor at your weekly meetings or in your workspaces? How does he do it? What is appropriate and what is not? Do you want to start each meeting with a joke? Could everyone take turns suggesting a fun activity?

Ask yourself often, "What am I doing to encourage a sense of fun and play in the workplace?" Here are some ideas to use. Pick the ones that would be appropriate to your organization.

- A manager in a government agency organized a hallway bowling tournament, and called a half-hour break for everyone to take turns participating while others covered the phones.

- Have a contest for the funniest cartoon. Encourage people to bring in cartoons for a week or two, post them and form a committee to judge them. Award small prizes like movie passes to the winner.

- Hold two-minute parades. Start a parade down the hall. Wind through all the offices and cubicles or even in the aisles of your store or the lobby of your building. Carry a portable boom box for music and encourage every-one to join in.

- As mentioned before, when a new employee joins the organization, pro-claim a day in their honor during the first week they are there. Put up signs in the bathrooms and elsewhere to let everyone know about it. Give them a special ribbon to wear on that day. Make a big deal of them and you will help that employee fit in faster and create a climate of retention.

- Name rooms, cubicles or halls after people. (It can change weekly or monthly.) Make up funny names for the rooms.

- Have an employee talent show during work hours, like lunch time, if possi-ble. If not, try after hours at a celebration of something like "we reached the end of the week" day.

- Bring in a comedian or humorist to speak during a brown-bag lunch. Or have each employee tell a favorite joke. Information off the Internet is okay too. (Put those funny e-mail jokes and stories you get to work.)

- Cover someone's work area with balloons for no reason at all.

- Proclaim a week in honor of "Tell someone they are doing a good job" and encourage everyone to do just that.

- Hold bingo games and give small prizes or actual money.

- Hold a party in the parking lot after work. Rent a popcorn machine and have decorations around a theme, like a beach party or a circus.

- Post everyone's baby pictures, from the CEO's on down. Have a contest to guess who they are.

- Award a "Mr. Potato Head" figure to the person who handled the most difficult customer that week.

- Start a "fun committee" to come up with even more ideas.

Even in times when a lot of people are searching for jobs, there are still many positions that are hard to fill. Many more businesses rely on entry-level people than ever before. There is a rapid expansion in quick service industries—all of them designed to employ large numbers of entry- and middle-management workers. Finding and retaining these workers is one key to customer service success.

Could any of these ideas, incorporating some to the five Rs, be useful in your business?

- Help people feel a sense of ownership in your company. Educate them in how to read your annual report and help them understand your financial goals and strategic plans. Then help them see that what they do fits into making these goals happen.

- Post scoreboards on these goals and keep them up all the time. Use sales goals, customer service goals and any other figures you can track on a weekly or monthly basis.

- Give praise. Ask supervisors and managers how often they give critical feedback versus positive reinforcement to their customer service workers. It should be three positive comments to every negative one.

- Develop employees' skills. Send them to a conference or trade show at your expense. It will keep them motivated about their job, and they will come back with some great ideas. The younger the worker, the more they will feel this is a "perk."

- Don't punish mistakes or employees will quickly lose all initiative and start to look elsewhere for a job. Coach them on what to do differently and celebrate what they just learned instead of punishing them.

- If you have more than one location, trade one employee for a week every once in awhile. Have them exchange ideas between the locations. It will make your employees feel valued—something that will help make them stay with you.

- Make sure everyone understands exactly what they are supposed to do. Provide a job description for every position in your company. Include the results expected from that job and then measure and reward them.

- Give your employees a "meeting free" day twice a month. Declare every other Friday a "no meeting day."

- Discourage anyone from calling your employees at night for business purposes. Evaluate whether everyone needs to wear a beeper or keep their cell phone on all the time. You need to give your employees some personal time where they cannot be contacted.

- Hold people accountable for some part of a project, no matter how small, and delegate authority as well as the task. People become energized and motivated when they feel they have control.

- Get together with each of your employees and write a development plan for them. Identify a strength or mid-range skill and develop a plan to make it stronger.

Quiz: The Eight Reasons People Leave

Are you guilty of any of these turnover accelerators? Check any that apply to your company.

_____ Poor compensation. You aren't on a level playing field as far as compensation is concerned. You must at least match what other companies in your industry pay.

_____ Poor benefits. Even though the cost of benefits is going up, it is still an important element in retention. Be sure yours measure up to your competitors'. And educate your employees as to what they are worth in terms of dollars they don't have to spend out of their own pockets.

_____ Lack of training. As mentioned above, if an employee doesn't understand all aspects of her job when she is asked to perform it, she will probably quit because of a lack of confidence.

_____ A toxic work environment. When an employee's workplace is filled with negative co-workers, a poor manager and politics, he will quickly become demotivated and leave.

_____ Lack of challenging job content. Boring, repetitious jobs are revolving-door jobs. Employees want some challenge in their jobs to keep them interested and learning.

_____ Lack of praise and recognition. As discussed in previous chapters, a climate of motivation and praise must be deeply rooted and something the company does often.

_____ Poor managers. Numerous research reports say that the number one reason that employees stay in their jobs is because of the skills of their managers.

Scoring

7-6: You probably have a good retention rate. Keep up the good work.

5-4: Your retention efforts could use some improvements. Try to institute some of the ideas from this chapter.

Less than 3: You are in trouble. If you can't retain your employees, you will never be able to use customer service as a competitive weapon.

CHAPTER THIRTEEN

Making This Work in Your Organization

Some business owners and managers are going to comprehend the issues in this book and others won't. Some will put it down and say, "It's too much trouble." But their businesses will suffer because the issue of customers wanting the value added by service is not going away. It will continue to grow in importance, especially in certain industries.

The processes described in this book may seem like a lot to consider in developing your customer service program, but it really isn't. Following this step-by-step guide will take less time than you think. Small and medium size businesses, by their very nature, can move faster and provide better service than their big business counterparts. They have the upper hand in capturing market share through exceptional customer service.

Remember: You can't just sit back and do what you have always done. You can't just put your people through a customer service training class and expect to have the kind of service that will make you extremely profitable. Things are changing. Customers are changing. You must change too. If you are to use customer service as your competitive edge, you must implement the steps in this book.

Customer service is the "ultimate marketing" according to Phillip Campbell, author of "Never Run Out of Cash". "It is harder and harder for companies to find the huge amount of money for advertising," he says. Campbell urges that word of mouth coming from good service and a good product are still the best and cheapest forms of advertising and marketing.

In many mature markets where there is minimal competitive advantage to be gained by product features or pricing, the quality of the service a business offers will continue to be one of the few potential differentiators available.

Forces That Will Affect Customer Service In The Future.

The future for customer service is not rosy. In fact, it will continue to be quite challenging. There are several forces at work that will make it hard for you to keep service levels high. Companies that succeed in achieving the levels of service that will positively affect their bottom line will take these factors into consideration and use the steps described in the book to overcome them.

Rising Customer Expectations

It's no secret that customer expectations are constantly escalating. They demand more every day. Every time a customer experiences superior customer service from a company, they expect to receive that same level of service elsewhere. "If they did it, why can't you," goes the thinking. It doesn't even have to be an experience with a direct competitor; it can be with any company.

Even while their expectations are being raised, customers are simultaneously becoming disheartened. They are finding service to be steadily declining—yet they keep hoping to find an oasis of service where they can gladly and happily spend their money. Your company needs to be that place, and it can be if you follow the advice in this book.

Continually getting feedback from your customers as to their expectations of your service and then making those expectations happen is critical to dealing with this challenge. If the customers' expectations are unreasonable, you must learn to manage those expectations by telling them up front what you can and can't do.

The Cranky Factor

In her book, *Why is Everyone So Cranky?* author Leslie Charles talks about America's "anger epidemic," where common courtesy is being abandoned. "They're in a huff and in a hurry," she says.

People aren't as nice as they used to be, and it is affecting customer service. Customers are harder to please and less willing to forgive a mistake. They are more likely to complain and to tell many of their friends and acquaintances about their poor service experience. They get angry and they rant and rave.

Make sure your employees receive training in dealing with those abusive customers. Provide a way for them to gracefully turn it over to a supervisor when it gets to be too much. Develop clearly defined policies and stick to them regarding customer returns and problem-solving.

Most of today's customers are time pressured and are trying to do more in less time, so when service takes longer than expected, they become difficult and take it out on the service provider. There's a reason why FedEx is so successful. Everyone wants it now. Customers don't want to stand in line anywhere. Not at the post office, gas pumps, or financial institutions. They are impatient and expect your service process to take this into consideration.

You need to look at your staffing, systems, procedures and processes in order to bring your service time down to its minimum.

And then there are the "terrorist customers" who are abusive to service providers and make unrealistic demands. They are out to take the company for all they can by whatever means. It is dangerous to develop restrictive rules to counter these terrorist customers because then all customers suffer. The customers you want to retain are turned off and they decide to take their business elsewhere.

Some customers deserve to be "fired," and a company with a true customer service culture realizes that they cannot make everyone happy. Especially the customers that are continually abusive to their employees. When you let a terrorist customer go, you are making a strong statement that you value your employees more than that one customer.

Too Few Employees Doing Too Much

Downsizing, right-sizing, pink-slipping. Whatever you call it, there are fewer people to do the work today. The average employee is doing the work of at least one former full-time employee who was laid off, and maybe even the work of a part-timer who was let go. They are stressed and depressed.

Connie Renfro, of St. Luke's Episcopal Hospital in the Texas Medical Center, likens this phenomenon to an orange that is squeezed until all the juice is gone—the juice that makes customer service happen. Drained service employees just go through the motions and don't deliver that extra discretionary effort that is essential to competitive-edge service.

The Echo Factor

Life is an echo; you get back what you send out. With all the cranky customers out there, service providers are taking more abuse than before. Is it any wonder that some of them snap back, no matter how much training they have in dealing with unhappy customers? Yet companies are requiring employees to be nice to customers at all costs, even if that customer is cursing and yelling.

Those same employees carry that stress home and take it out on their families. This leads to a lower retention rate, as employees decide that the job is just not worth it.

Your business needs to be aware of this challenge and continue to use the motivation techniques discussed in this book to keep your customer service employees from burning out. Give employees time off from the front lines every once in a while, so they can recharge their batteries.

The High-Tech Tangle

Customer service is being transformed by continual innovations in technology. The Internet is constantly adding ways to contact, serve and sell to customers. It lowers communication costs and increases the information flow. The customer service employee of the future will need to be very proficient in all the technologies that make customer service happen.

Make sure that your employees are very well trained in the technology your company uses and resist the urge to sit them down in front of a computer terminal with minimal instruction.

But how far can technology go? Many people complain because they cannot reach a "real person" or they get caught in "technology hell," either online or in a tangled automated routing system that cannot answer their particular questions. Many times the technology results in far more aggravation than service and leaves the customer extremely dissatisfied. The companies that continue to be successful will use technology as only part of the service mix. You need to be able to do business with your customers across all channels and deliver service anytime, 24/7, anywhere, while also offering the option to reach a live person.

The "Death Spiral" of Customer Service

It starts at the top, with owners and managers signaling right and turning left. "The customer is everything," they say. Meanwhile, they cut staff so it is impossible to serve the customer well, or they trim inventory so much that customers can no longer find what they want.

The spiral continues as owners make it difficult for the customer to contact the company by using the aforementioned tangle of technology. The customer ends up angry, frustrated and unhappy. The customer support department is a maze of telephones, Web sites, punch one for this, two for that, unanswered e-mail and other barriers. The customer is left feeling that he is not important, because the systems are all made for the company's benefit, not the customers'.

Owners and managers often let their customers abuse the customer service representatives and don't stand up for their employees when customers are unreasonable in their demands. Employees, in turn, deliver rude and unsatisfactory service to customers, who become even more abusive to those same employees. And the spiral continues until the company goes out of business and the owner wonders why.

In order for your company to avoid the death spiral you must work to develop a true customer service culture. One that can deliver competitive-edge service over and over again, customer after customer. The pressures on small and medium size businesses are not going away: large companies will continue to threaten with low prices and a gigantic selection, and customers will continue to demand service value in their transactions.

Use the information in this book to avoid the death spiral of customer service. Start by understanding where your organization is now and where you want it to go. But realize that it won't happen overnight. And remember that customer service has moved from simple training and "smile" classes to an organization-wide effort with many steps.

Then focus on a few goals at a time. Persistence is the key to great customer service. Start by working toward a few goals that are easily obtainable, and then build on those successes. This will create the momentum and motivation to continue your efforts.

Customers today are evermore demanding—an organization cannot wait and take its time creating exceptional service. It must happen now. If you want to have competitive-edge service that gives you an advantage in the marketplace, if you want people to select your company over all others, use the information in this book to develop a strategy that will result in outstanding customer service.

APPENDIX A

Sample Training Program

Here is a sample training program to use in developing your own approach. It is based on the five things all people want and need in order to feel they have received excellent customer service. All of them overlap somewhat, and if your employees deliver one out of the five, then some of the other wants and needs are also being accomplished. For instance, when you make your customers feel welcome, it also makes them feel comfortable that they are going to receive good service. This program encompasses training in both technical and interpersonal behavioral skills.

Think of a time when you took some friends to your favorite restaurant. In the past it has been a wonderful experience and you want to share it with friends. But when you arrived, there was no hostess to greet you. You waited for about five minutes before anyone approached you. She did not smile or make you feel welcome. In fact, she made you feel like you were an interruption in her day. Because you were not made to feel welcome, you also started to feel uncomfortable about inviting your friends to accompany you. You began to question whether this was the right choice. You also didn't feel important because you were not greeted promptly. See how it goes?

Here are the five elements all people want and need, with a little explanation about each. Use this basic outline to customize a program for your organization. Briefly explain each of the needs and then ask your employees to describe how they make them happen in their jobs. You could do one element a week.

1. Make me feel welcome.

2. Make me feel listened to.

3. Make me feel important and valued.

4. Keep me informed.

5. Make me feel comfortable with your service.

1. **Make me feel welcome.** When you make a customer feel welcome with a warm greeting on the phone or a smile and good eye contact in person, you

are setting the stage for the customer to experience good customer service. The number-one signal that someone is welcome is a smile—a real one, not an "on stage" smile. It has to reach the eyes and genuinely say, "I'm glad you're here. I remember that you are my paycheck."

Eye contact is also important. In America, looking someone in the eyes is a signal that I am listening to you, I notice you, or you are important to me. This is not true for all cultures, so you need to be sensitive to that, but the majority of your customers want good eye contact.

Positive body language is still another factor. When you cross your arms at your first meeting with a customer, it erects an invisible barrier that the customer subconsciously senses. But when you lean forward and keep your palms up and open, it says, "I can be trusted."

And what about the telephone? Does your voice say, "I wish this phone would stop ringing," when you answer it? Or does your voice have a smile that makes your customer or internal coworker customer feel welcome?

Acknowledging them quickly is another way to say, "Welcome!" I'm sure you have experienced the way not to do it. You walk into a store and the salesclerks are too busy talking to each other to even notice you, much less ask if they can help you. Or you're at the grocery store checkout, and the cashier and the bagger are so busy chatting about their weekend that you feel like an unwanted guest. They look at you as if they hope you will go away and quit bothering them.

A bank established a policy where the minute a customer crossed a certain marking on the carpet, he was to be greeted. Even if it was simply a nod and a wave. What service targets can you set to make sure your customers feel welcome each time?

2. **Make me feel listened to.** When you listen to a customer and, therefore, make them feel that you understand their need or problem, they will become very loyal to you and your business. Often, all an angry customer wants is to feel that they have been listened to. Listening to someone makes them feel that they are important.

In order for customers to feel listened to and understood, you must use good listening skills and probe to determine their needs and desires. You must listen for the feelings communicated as well as the content of the customer's message.

The first step in making a customer feel that you are listening to them is to use "whole body" listening. That means you look them in the eyes and give them your full attention. No fidgeting or continuing to work on the computer. In person, nod your head occasionally to let them know you are listening or tilt your head, also a sign of listening. By all means, avoid closed body language like crossed arms or not fully facing the person.

On the telephone, you need to give some meaningless words, grunts and phrases like "uh-huh," "go on" or anything that lets your customer know you are listening. Don't shuffle papers, work on the computer or anything else that will make your customer feel less than listened to.

Another way to let your customer know that you are listening to them is to paraphrase some of what they have said. This is a great way to check to make sure you really understand the customer. Use phrases like, "If I understand you correctly..." "Sounds like you are concerned about..." or "Are you saying that...?" This will encourage feedback from your customer.

Take notes when appropriate. This is a very visual sign to your customer that you are really listening to what they have to say and value it. It will also help calm an irate customer. When you seem concerned enough to write what the customer is saying, it really makes him feel you value his thoughts and concerns.

Asking questions is another way to assure your customers that you are listening to them and trying to understand what they need. This can help you clarify the details and check to make sure that you and the customer are on the same page.

3. **Make me feel important.** Making your customers feel that you are glad they have chosen to do business with you is another thing that is important to do for every customer every time. A lot of companies do not do a good job of this.

Surely you've experienced the scenario of a customer service representative asking you, "What can I do for you," in a tone of voice that is really saying, "Hurry up!" All these things add up to a customer feeling that you don't really want their business and that they are unimportant.

Making your customers feel that they matter to your business is a critical part of giving good customer service. If they don't feel that you value them, they will quickly take their business somewhere else and tell all their friends why they did so.

Here are some ideas to help you make all your customers feel important:

- First, use their name if possible. Often you can get this off a credit card. Then remember that name if he or she is a regular customer. If you deal with customers mostly on the telephone, try to recognize their voices. Never use their first name unless told by the customer to do so.

- Be sure to look them in the eyes and sincerely say, "How may I help you," with a big smile. As mentioned earlier, if you remember that every customer is your paycheck, it will be easier to do. Eye contact is also a critical part of making the customer feel important.

A department store manager would silently say about every customer who came into his department, "Hello groceries, hello rent check, hello utilities." That reminded him that helping these customers helped to pay his bills.

- Don't forget about your internal customers—your coworkers. They also deserve to be made to feel important, so check yourself to see if you are doing these things for them too.

- Another technique to make your customers feel important is to use "pedestal words." Those are words that do just that—put your customers up on a pedestal. They are words like "Please," "Thank you," "I'd appreciate it if you would..." and "May I please...?"

- Give the customer your undivided attention. Don't continue what you are doing and finish that before you greet the customer. The customer is the most important thing in the world to you—not finishing your paperwork. Don't eat or chew gum when you are speaking to customers on the telephone or in person. This will give a bad impression.

- When a customer wants something that is a little outside the policies and rules of your organization, try to show some flexibility. You don't need to "give away the store," but try to bend a little to make your customer happy.

This will also make them feel important.

The Persona Day Spa has a strict four-hour cancellation policy on their services. If the client doesn't cancel her appointment four hours before her scheduled time, she will be billed for the service. The spa owner knows how important it is to bend a little with their clients, so the first time the client forgets to cancel, a letter is written explaining their policy and saying they will waive it this first time, but will not be able to do it in the future. This does two things: it reminds the client of the policy and makes them feel important, because the spa has made an exception in their case.

Above all—be responsive. Return calls and e-mails quickly. This also sends a strong message that the customer is important.

Another contributor to your customer's feeling important is your accessibility. Are your hours of operation customer friendly? Do you realize that your customers need time before and after regular work hours to access your services? Or are you like the physician's office staff who shuts down at lunchtime for an hour and a half to two hours? Too bad this is the only time you can call to make an appointment or ask a question. Their lunch hour is more important than you.

The last time you were in a large store looking for something you didn't know where to find, did an employee stop what he was doing and approach you to ask if he could help you? If so, that probably made you feel important.

4. **Keep me informed.** You can keep your customers informed in many ways. Suppose you promise information to a customer by a certain time. When that time arrives and you still don't have all the information, you call them back to give a status report.

Or if you have an appointment with someone and you are running late, call to tell her and to give a new estimated time of arrival. Don't you wish more repair people would do this? How many times have you been told that someone will be there between 9:00 am and noon and then no one shows? And worse, no one bothers to call.

The lack of courtesy also makes the customer feel unimportant. It is just as if a customer representative said, "You are not important enough for us to take the time to call you back." Does that make for loyal and committed customers who give you lots of referrals? Of course not.

A chemical company's customer service representatives were very good about letting their customers know when a shipment might be late. Each morning the representatives checked the delivery schedules to make sure they were going to meet the deadlines for delivery. If not, they would immediately call the customer to alert them and to discuss a new delivery time. In this way, the plants they supplied were better able to manage production and to avoid shutdowns that could cost millions of dollars.

A garage door opener company has been very successful because they have a telephone receptionist who can talk knowledgeably to potential customers about the openers they sell. She is able to intelligently discuss the features and benefits of the different brands instead of having to say, "I don't know," and wait to reach a technician who can answer the questions. By informing her customers, she is not only answering that need, but she is also making them feel comfortable that they will continue to receive good service.

5. **Make me feel comfortable with your service.** Making your customer feel comfortable is a lot more than offering them a cup of coffee and a place to sit down. It is an indefinable feeling that they have chosen the right company to do business with. Comfort is a feeling you provide that assures customers you will follow through with what you say. It is honesty, integrity and a feeling of trust about the product and service you offer.

It is anticipating the needs, desires and questions of your customers. Customer service representatives have studied the most frequently asked questions and know the answers. For instance, the receptionists at one doctor's office were often asked the location of the bus stop. Now, that certainly wasn't a medical question, but the employees took it upon themselves to learn where it was so they could serve their patients better. They also printed a list of most frequently asked questions about certain medical procedures they provided. Not only did this make the patient feel more comfortable, but it also saved the staff time. When you do these things, customers feel more comfortable about all of your services.

Here are a few more ways to foster a feeling of comfort:

- Maintain privacy and confidentiality. If the customer's check has just been rejected by your verification service, don't announce it to everyone else in line. Take them out of earshot to discuss it.

- The professional look of your place of business is another key in making your customers feel comfortable. If it is dirty and ill-maintained, your customers will transfer that to your service or product and feel uncomfortable about doing business with you.

- Is your staff appropriately dressed for your business? A car mechanic would wear a different outfit than a banker, of course, but each of them would need to be in neat, well-fitting clothing appropriate to the job. If something is wrong or unprofessional-looking about their outfit, the customer often will feel uncomfortable about your service or product. They think, "After all, if you can't get basic stuff like that right, how can you satisfy my needs?"

- Honest answers, pressure-free selling, business conducted in a language free of jargon and having the information and answers that your customers want are other ways to fill your customers' needs for comfort.

Even the city where you live should offer a level of service that makes you feel comfortable. Are the police readily accessible and responsive to your concerns about people speeding on your street, for instance? Is your trash picked up in a timely manner? Can you reach the city's departments quickly? Are the city employees friendly and eager to solve your problem or listen to your concerns? When these things happen again and again, they will all add to your feeling of comfort that you have chosen the right place to live.

What about your telephone system? Is it a maze of "push one for this, push two for that" that causes your customers to get lost forever? That will make your customers feel uncomfortable, and they will probably visit your competitors to see if they are easier to access.

Responsiveness is still another indicator as to whether customers will feel comfortable about doing business with you. As mentioned above, returning phone calls and e-mails promptly is critical. How long does it take you to get back to a customer with a complaint?

Don't forget your internal customers! When a coworker needs information from you in order to do their job, do you get back to them in a timely manner? Or do you say, "Oh, she's not a customer. She's just someone I work with."

Developing a comfort level in your customers is an important part of achieving superior customer service. When your customers feel comfortable about your business, they will become more loyal and refer it to others.

Constant, intensive and universal training is a hallmark of companies that produce great customer service. Exceptional customer service cannot happen unless you train for it to happen... continuously. You can't just conduct minimal training at the start of the job and then check it off the list. You must be constantly training and retraining your employees if you hope to deliver the kind of service that will give you the competitive-edge. Use this program to keep the subject of service constantly in front of your employees.

APPENDIX B

How to Conduct Your Own Customer Panel

Here is a step-by-step process for conducting your own customer panel. You don't need a fancy room with a two-way mirror. All you need is a room, flip charts, colored paper, marking pens, masking tape and some chairs!

Purpose of Panels:

To determine your customer's expectations. To determine how well your customer's expectations are being met in the area of service. To then use that information to improve service levels.

Makeup of Panel:

Usually two hours in length, with approximately 12-14 people. Key people or the entire staff from the area being discussed will also attend and observe, but will not participate unless asked a direct question.

Steps:

1. Develop a list of customers you would like to participate. Choose a cross section of some who are extremely important to you, some that have had problems, and those who you feel will not be shy in sharing their opinions. To get the final number of approximately 14 participants, you usually need to develop a list of at least 22 possible participants. Call some of them, tell them what you are doing and get feedback from them as to the best time and place for the panels to take place.

2. Decide on the date and time, based on that information. Make arrangements. It is always good to have some refreshments and a small gift for the participants if possible.

3. Room requirements for the panel: You will need a room large enough to have tables and chairs for the participants, chairs and a table at the back of the room for the observers from the department being discussed and two flip charts to capture comments. The room also needs to be one where papers can be taped to the walls.

4. Invite the participants. You can do it formally through the mail, via e-mail, or by telephone. The method depends on how much time you have to assemble the panel and what you think is the best way to communicate with them.

5 Send confirmation correspondence to participants with details of where, when, etc.

6. Two days before the event, call (don't e-mail) to reconfirm. This is a critical step.

7. After all the participants are assembled, give each participant a stack of 8½ x 11-inch brightly colored paper and a marking pen.

8. State what you would like to learn from them. This is called the "task statement." For instance, "What are we doing well," "What are we doing not so well" and other factors you would like to learn about your service. Use the questions discussed earlier, and paste the questions on the wall or write them on the flip chart.

9. Then, using the marking pens, have the participants generate one idea per piece of paper on that statement. Encourage them to be specific. Don't let them say, "You are offering good customer service," for instance. Have them write exactly what they like about your service. Are the personnel friendly, is the service fast, do they like the food?

10. Give them ten minutes to generate as many ideas as possible relating to that one question; then paste each statement on the wall. Masking tape usually works well.

11. Now you want to discuss their ideas. Group similar ideas together. Put all comments about food together, all comments about speed of service together and so on.

12. As you are doing this, ask questions about anything that is not clear and jot any additional information on the flip chart or directly on the original piece of paper.

13. Repeat the process for as many questions as you have time.

14. Thank everyone, give them their gifts for reimbursement and let them go. Be sure to stay within the stated time frame. Never run overtime!

15. After the event, write a thank you letter to all participants.

Then make sure you use this information to improve your service.

APPENDIX C

REVIEW GAMES

Quiz show review game

- Divide the orientation group into two teams and have each team develop three to five questions based on material covered in the orientation. You can increase the number of questions if you have more time or have covered a lot of material.

- Have each team select a leader to ask and answer the questions from the other team. (Everyone on the team can have input into the answers, though.) Be sure to enforce the rule that only the leader can speak to the other team, or you will have chaos with everyone shouting the answers.

- Announce that you will be the ultimate judge on whether an answer is correct.

- Taking turns, each team asks the other to answer one of their questions.

- If the answering team gets the answer correct, they get one point.

- If it is incorrect, they lose a point.

- Award prizes to the team with the most points.

- This quiz will let you see if any of the information you shared didn't get through or if employees are not clear about the answer. You can use the quiz to alert you about what you need to go over again.

Question matching

Write a series of review questions about the material you have covered in the customer service training course. Cut them into individual strips of paper. Then write the answers to those questions on another piece of paper and cut those into strips. Give the question strips to half the class and the answer strips to the other half of the class. Participants circulate and match up the questions and the answers. As soon as they have matched all their questions and answers, they sit down. You can make a contest out of it with prizes to the people who complete the activity the fastest.

INDEX

A

Customer Service: How to Do It Right!

Customer Service: How to Do It Right!

F

G

P

at returns department, 40–41
rudeness to customers, 35, 74, 154
Porter, Michael, 28
praise for employees, 138, 141–44, 183, 185
and slacking off, 143
written, 140, 143
Premier Company, The, 126
pressure-free selling, 198
price
profit (See profit)
service vs., 6, 10, 17–19, 23
value and (See value)
pride in work, 67
PRIDE Program (Personal Responsibility In Delivering Excellence), 138
privacy:
customer, 198
for employee coaching, 160
"problem customers," 91, 187–88, 189
problems, customer. See complaints, customer; unhappy customers
problems, employee, 8, 154–66
demotivators (See demotivators for employees)
poor service (See poor service)
problem-solving, 88–91. See also specific problem descriptions
ability, as job requirement, 98
empowering employees for (See empowering your staff)
"fixing" the person first, 83–88
procedures, systems and. See rules
productivity, standards for, 176
products and services:
offering large range, 26
professionalism, 198
profit:
customer retention and, 6
exceptional service and, 22
Pryor Report, 113
"push my button" letter, 80
Putt-Putt FunHouse, 66–67, 79, 101, 104, 179–80

Q

quality, 27
Quest Business Agency, 139
questionnaires, customer. See surveys
questions, interview. See under interviewing job candidates: questions, appropriate
quiz show review game, 202
quizzes. See checklists; surveys; tests

R

teaching new employees, 116
unnecessary, 149
"unwritten," company, 115

S

Notes

Notes